Lest We Forget...
The Melungeon Colony of Newman's Ridge

Jim Callahan

The Overmountain Press

JOHNSON CITY, TENNESSEE

ISBN: 1-57072-167-X

234567890

Contents

Introduction

Lest We Forget is a history of a much maligned group of dark, Mediterranean-like people called Melungeons. They are investigated in detail, from their many surprising souces of origin to their eventual colony in the Newman's Ridge area of Hancock County, Tennessee. The author has unique insights into their true story as he is a direct descendant of most of the core group. He has the skill and background to be on the outside looking in, as well as the personal relationships to extract direct and personal knowledge from relatives and associates of the group.

These elusive people exist in many pockets throughout the southeastern United States, but this one area contains the most well-known and studied representative example of the people. The rugged terrain helped contribute to this concentrated racial isolate that has long attracted scholars into their area for study.

Their isolation on Newman's Ridge and Vardy Valley eventually resulted in an interest and long-term commitment from Presbyterian missionaries from New York. The missionaries stayed long enough to record histories and to educate, teaching agriculture, home economics, hygiene, and, particularly, pride and self-worth. After almost 100 years of successes, the missionaries were no longer needed, as the colony had been dispersed and only a memory remained of the unique isolate.

Only a semblance remains of this once-concentrated group of dark people, but the author has followed the theories of their role in the settlement of America through the history of their decline. He concludes optimistically, following them back toward a new place in our history, as they enter a period of their revival and the preservation of a lost heritage. He has devoted many years to researching the clan and feels a deep sense of love and affection for his people.

Chapter 1
The Search for Origin

This is a twofold story: one part of origin and the other of discrimination. How little we know or understand of our origin and early history! How subtle is the mask of discrimination; so hidden that we are unaware of its effect on our lives. We have always been an inquisitive species, but animal instincts, bias, living only for the present, or missing records frequently overcome our ability to accept or analyze gaps and behaviors in our knowledge of the past.

This presentation will deal with the possibility that one of the first boat people to reach North America was different than recorded. Their subsequent rejection by neighbors will be covered at appropriate times throughout this story of their lives. This minor group appears as a result of various unexplained, unknown, or unreported incidents in the exploration and settlement of our lands. They were not generally acknowledged as possible contributors to the settlement of America by the authors of accepted Anglo-Saxon history books. They do occasionally appear and disappear in writings as unexplained, unimportant entities by a few speculative historians. Early westward immigrants encountering them for the first time probably labeled them half-breeds or mulattos. Later, to their dismay, they were called Melungeons. On the following page is a female example of the generalized appearance of these people.

Even the accepted origin of the name, Melungeon, is a mystery. Those thinking the French language was a link to their origin used the French word *melange*, or mixture, to describe them. Those choosing the Greek language used the word *melos*, or melanism, for dark. As the people themselves claimed to be Portuguese, scholars have looked at the word *melungo*, the Afro-Portuguese word for shipmate.[1]

A less popular term, but perhaps as important in the study of their history and demise, is the Middle English term *mal engine*, which means treacherous and deceitful. Others use terms such as

Today's Melungeon.
Courtesy of Isa Mae Collins McCay (deceased). Tammy Glass.

"mal Injun," a distortion of bad Indian, or "mal urgent," describing a distinctive bad smell attributed to Melungeons.[2] These latter terms are certainly discriminatory, and, as we examine their story, we will find many more instances of discrimination that could have resulted in the mystery of their place in history, as well as their unaccepted name.

More recent speculation proposed a name of Moorish or Turkish origin. The Turkish derivation is from the words *melon* (cursed) and *can* (soul). Together, these words are pronounced *melun-jun* or cursed soul, "one who has been abandoned by God." The Turks were reported to have these thoughts about sailors, for they frequently disappeared without a trace and never returned home.[3] Past researchers may have perceived their origin with limited facts, then searched their own language for a word that might be similar to the word "Melungeon."

We will not attempt to cover here all of the many possible group connections of the Melungeons or any other unknown North American heritages, as many people have their own missing or hidden stories. Possibly the French, Spanish, Negro, Lumbee, Croatian, Redbone, and various Native American tribes were more involved than currently accepted with segments of the gene pool that contributed to our country. We will concentrate only on information about this one group, in an attempt to cover theories of the Melungeons being from another continent and present in North America prior to 1492, to more recent theories of their being a local mixture or a triracial isolate.

The present remnants of Melungeons live in several isolated areas in Western Virginia, North Carolina, Eastern Tennessee, and Kentucky, as well as several other less-identified areas of the United States. We will devote most our time to analyzing the Melungeons of East Tennessee for two reasons: first — the author is the son of a Melungeon from that area, second — the people of this area have been researched more than others, and more materials telling their story are available for scrutiny and speculation. This investigation is limited geographically, but eventually, even small probes in this one area may heighten our awareness of the many areas of unsolved mysteries — including links to behaviors in all our pasts.

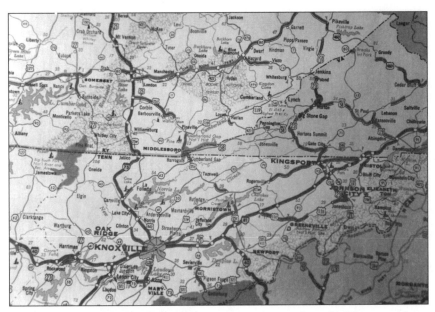

Map Of The Melungeon Area. A longtime concentration of Melungeons have been identified in this general area.

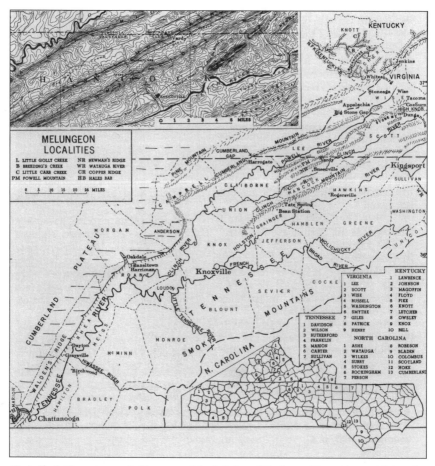

Detailed County and Topographical Map Of Area Counties within the designated Melungeon area of the study. Courtesy of Dr. Edward T. Price and Geographical Review.

Map of Vardy Area - A Melungeon Community in the valley between Newman's Ridge and Powell Mountain. Note early concentration of houses in this narrow valley. No reliable road was built into this remote area until the 1930s. Sketch courtesy of Macie Mullins.(Not to scale)

Detailed Map of Vardy around Presbyterian Missionary School. Ibid

Early road over Newman's Ridge to the isolated Vardy Valley. Photo Courtesy of Ellen Trent (deceased) David Trent.

[1]Jean Patterson Bible, *Melungeons Yesterday And Today*, East Tennessee Printing Company,1975, p. 11
[2]Lee Anne Allen, "Introduction To Melungeon Bibliography," *Tennessee Folklore Society Bulletin*, Murfreesboro, 1992, p. 122.
[3]Stephen Munsey, "Melungeons provide link between Wise County, Turkey," *Bristol Herald Courier*, October 14, 1995, p. 1.

Chapter 2
Physical Characteristics

An examination of the many descriptions attributed to Melungeons could begin from information recorded several hundred years ago, but time adds to speculation of whether the earlier writers are speaking of this particular group of people. For example, in 1673, a young Englishman by the name of James Needham was employed by Abraham Wood to penetrate the land of mystery beyond the mountain chains in Virginia. Needham departed from the Wood trading post at the northern end of the Catawba-Occaneeci trail with Gabriel Arthur, "who was probably an indentured servant of Wood," and eight Indians.[1] His assignment was to discover the Valley of the Tennessee and the domain of the Overhill Cherokees for the English, so far as was known. No detail was spared as the small party moved westward. Eventually, they visited the Tomahitan Cherokees, thought to be a remnant of the Mohetans from the New River of Virginia. The New River area and environs have been theorized by some as a pathway for many later Melungeons, which will be considered later in this study.

Analysis of a letter implies the small group reached what is now known as East Tennessee, eventually finding some non-Native Americans. To quote: "Eight dayes jorny down this river lives a white people which have long beardes and whiskers and weares clothing, and on some of ye other rivers lives a hairey people."[2] One person was left with the newly discovered people to learn their language as the others departed toward home for a return later.

It was recorded that, "Ye white people have a bell which is six feet over which they ring morning and evening and att that time a great number of people congregate together and talkes he knowes not what."[3] Some modern-day writers speculate this brief physical description was of some early Melungeons. Others theorize the white people around the bell ultimately called themselves by the surname of Bell. The name Bell is still common in the Melungeon area.

In 1872, the Judge Lewis Shepard case of Hamilton County, Tennessee, influenced many of the early physical descriptions of the Melungeons. The case was very colorful and involved a wealthy man and his family, including slaves, that migrated from Virginia to Tennessee. Eventually the man died, leaving a widow and three sons. Later, two of the sons died without wives or heirs. The one surviving brother eventually inherited all his father's assets.

This surviving son, then living in Rossville (now known as Chattanooga), had some temporary mental problems caused by fever, but recovered and continued to manage the farms from town, with the assistance of a farm tenant. After a time, the young absentee landlord fell in love with one of his tenant's daughters. The daughter was described as, "famed for her beauty, grace, manner, and modesty. She was a dark brunette with a suite of black hair, which was coveted by all the girls who knew her. Her form was petite, and yet, was so plump and so well developed as to make her a irresistibly charming young woman. She was most beautiful of face, and had a rich black eye, in whose depths the sunbeams seemed to gather. When she loosed her locks they fell, almost reaching the ground, and shone in the sunlight, or quivered like the glamour which the full moon throws on the placid water. She was the essence of grace and loveliness."[4]

The young landowner and the lovely girl applied for a marriage license, but were obstructed by his remarried mother and a half-sister on grounds that he was mentally incompetent from his earlier fever to marry. They also charged an illegality to the marriage with the girl on the grounds of an interracial union. The resourceful young man scurried over the state line into Georgia and was married on June 14, 1856.

The young couple bore a son who died in infancy and, subsequently, a daughter in 1858. The young mother died eight days after the birth of her daughter, and her husband became violently insane. The man was taken into protective custody and kept under guard for a long time. He did not recover his faculties but improved enough to be deemed harmless. He moved back into his home and functioned with the assistance of a guardian, Mr. Foust.

Upon returning home, he developed a strange set of routines, such as a morning plunge in the nearby creek, even through the ice in winter. He plucked all the hairs from his body as any appeared. From this idiosyncrasy, it would seem logical that he would not have been a man heavily endowed with hair. (Perhaps a differentiating clue?) Along with these strange habits, many, many cats were kept in the house to ward off evil spirits.

The saga continued as the incompetent man, unable to manage his parental affairs, had his mother and half-sisters intervene to send his one survivor, the daughter, off to the swamps of southern Illinois with a maternal aunt. Aunt Betsy was solicited by either treats or bribes to take the infant and never return. She fled in haste with her young niece, but was thoughtful enough to carry the family Bible with her, which contained a record of this man's marriage and the birth of his two children.

A Mr. Samuel Williams followed the plight of the young girl and instructed Aunt Betsy to keep in contact with him. He sensed that someday there would be a contest for the distribution of the incompetent man's assets.

Eventually, Mr. Foust, the guardian, allowed the dependent man to live in his own home, with one of the tenants perpetually available for all his food and daily needs. Mr. Foust was held in high esteem in the community and invested the land rents wisely, accumulating many secured funds for his dependent ward.

Many years later, in 1872, the remaining two half-sisters and the heir of the deceased half-sister reappeared to sue Mr. Foust for wasteful management and irresponsible guardianship of their half-brother. They produced falsified statements as they attempted to prove mismanagement, wasted assets, and wasted loans to insolvent persons. The suit also declared their half-brother to be an incurable and permanent lunatic, rarely having a lucid interval. Based on such an impossible situation, the sisters stated an immediate need to assume responsibility of the estate. They agreed to provide bond and surety for all the needs of the unfortunate brother.

Fortunately, the two persons held as sureties on the bond of guardianship by the guardian of the estate felt responsible. One of the persons on the bond was Mr. Samuel Williams who, as mentioned previously, was concerned about the future of Aunt Betsy and her young niece. The suit named the sureties as responsible for honoring the details of the decree, and they responded with vigor as they began to search for a lawyer. It seemed that all the local lawyers were already committed to the opposition.

After an anxious period, a young, inexperienced lawyer by the name of S. Lewis Shepard was hired by Mr. Williams to prove the girl was the legal heir of the mentally unbalanced man. Mr. Williams agreed to serve in the capacity of next friend to the missing and forgotten girl and to be responsible for all costs. Mr. Williams presented the court with the new proposal naming the exiled child the sole heir of the demented man, with stipulations for her care and education. The document stated that her education had been sadly neglected during her imposed exile.

This new revelation hit the community like a bolt of lightning followed by a clap of thunder out of a clear blue sky. The sisters denied all the facts presented about a supposed girl heir living in exile in Illinois. They denied the girl's existence and the legitimacy of her father's marriage with believable reasons.

Mr. Williams departed to Illinois, attempting to bring the girl and the family Bible back as defense against the suit. After considerable persuasion, he convinced Aunt Betsy to release the girl to his custody along with the family Bible. Aunt Betsy was also promised a delayed, safe return to Tennessee after she disposed of her assets. This request was later honored by Mr. Williams.

The young girl was fifteen years of age when she returned to the home of her birth to battle for her inheritance. She had lived a very primitive lifestyle on the banks of the Mississippi with her Aunt Betsy. They had cut wood to supply passing steamboats and tilled small patches for sustenance farming. The girl did not need or know of proper dress. She was uncouth and unsophisticated, straight from the backwoods, but she possessed a beautiful, dark face and a figure that showed the potential of pleasing the most fastidious.

The trial was highly visible in the area, with sixty depositions taken on various issues raised in the proceedings. The first issue in the trial was the actuality of the marriage. There was no problem establishing the marriage of the man and woman, as witnesses to the marriage and the official in charge were still living. The record in the family Bible established the date of birth of the contested heir.

The challenge by the sisters of the capability of the half-brother to have been a part of a legal marriage was deemed invalid. The judge mandated that only one of a pair can rule on a marriage contract, and such contracts cannot be attacked collaterally.

The key issue of the trial was a statute in Tennessee prohibiting the intermarriage of a white with a person of Negro blood to the sixth degree. It was alleged that the mother of the girl had Negro blood within the prohibited degree. The evidence established the family of this woman was in no way connected with the Negro race. Her people were described as about the color of a mulatto with high foreheads, long, straight black hair, high cheekbones, thin lips, small feet with high insteps, and prominent Roman noses. It was added that the features of the Negro and mulatto were the opposite of those described.

The trial considered the issue of whether the original tenant, Mr. Bolton, father of the deceased mother in question, had served in the War of 1812. The records showed he had applied earlier and was rejected for a pension for serving as a soldier in the war. At the time of his supposed enlistment, Negroes and mulattos could not serve in the army as soldiers. These minorities had been known to serve in lesser military capacities such as cooks or teamsters, but not soldiers. The old tenant could not recall any evidence to confirm his military service, but he had been heard by others repetitively singing some sort of a list of men. Apparently, he had heard the list repeated daily at military roll call while serving in his regiment. He could not remember the company number, but his recall of a sing-song of names led to an extensive search in the War Department in Washington. As luck would have it, the court was able to legitimize him as a former enlisted soldier.

Another ploy of the opposition was to prove that all the Bolton family were kinky-headed Negroes. Some older Negro witnesses were introduced to confirm the kinkiness of the hair of the family. The witnesses confirmed that all the daughters had kinky hair, including the guardian, Aunt Betsy, and the mother of the girl in question. None of the witnesses knew that Aunt Betsy was still alive and had been caring for the child in Illinois. Aunt Betsy was served a deposition the following Saturday, and she cut a lock of hair to pin to the deposition from her coal black hair. She pulled out an old-fashioned tucking comb and reached to her top knot to separate a straight, black strand four feet long. The strand was perfectly free from kink or any tendency to curl.

For additional proof, Judge Shepard gave an eloquent plea, in the old-fashioned oratory of the period, as he reiterated the characteristics of these people and described them as a particular race not even remotely allied to Negroes. He described them as descendants of Carthage of ancient Phoenicia. He continued by saying that they had fled across the Straits of Gibraltar after being defeated by the Romans, to live for a period in Portugal. He reiterated how these same people fought bravely and heroically in the Punic Wars. He told of their women even cutting their long black hair in order for the state to have it braided and twisted into cables with which to fasten their galleys and ships of war to the shore.[5]

He stated that a considerable body of these people had migrated to South Carolina at the time of the Revolutionary War to settle near the North Carolina line. He told of them living in the area for several years before being discriminated against as mulattos or free Negroes. At the time, they were ostracized by neighbors, commanded to attend Negro schools, and admitted to white churches on the footing of Negroes.

He testified that South Carolina had a law taxing free Negroes at a rate per capita and that they were always able to avoid the tax. Eventually, they tired of the continual bad treatment and migrated once again, to the mountains of East Tennessee, later spreading westward to the site of the trial.

Judge Shepard added additional proof of race as he stated Bolton had voted in the county as white since his arrival and had testified in court. Neither of these rights were freedoms of Negroes.

Other evidence included by the judge was a tragic past murder of one of Bolton's grandchildren by a white man. Bolton prosecuted the man, but the defendant filed a plea in abatement, stating Bolton was a Negro with no right to prosecute. The jury found the plea to be false, convicted the defendant, and sent him to prison for a long term.

The eventual decree was in favor of the girl as the heir apparent of her father. She was to be educated and supported out of his estate and to inherit the estate after his death. The outcome of this case influenced the outcome of many Melungeon cases in the courts for many years after the final decision.[6]

Moving forward to 1889, we find another example of documented, written identification of the people. Swan M. Burnett, M.D., at the Anthropological Society of Washington, identified them as dark, but not the same hue as mulatto. He stated that their hair may be either straight or wavy, and some were described as having high cheekbones. He described the men as straight, large, and fine-looking. He mentioned only one older female appearing hag-like.[7]

In the same presentation, Dr. Burnett stated a number of Melungeons were challenged in the courts during the period of time before the Civil War about their right to vote due to their skin color and flat footedness. The court members were allowed to examine the feet of the people. One subject was thought to be sufficiently flat-footed to be deprived of suffrage. The other four or five were considered to have sufficient arch and, therefore, white blood, to be allowed to vote.[8]

A few years later, in 1891, a female by the name of Will Allen Dromgoole spent a considerable amount of time living among the Melungeons. She described them as having reddish-brown complexion, totally unlike mulattos. She described the men as very tall and straight with small, sharp eyes and high cheekbones. She mentioned their straight black hair, which was worn rather long. She noted that the women were smaller than the average white woman, with black hair and eyes, high cheekbones, and the same reddish-brown complexion. The hands of the women were quite shapely and pretty. She even observed the female feet as short and shapely despite the women being constantly barefooted on steep, rocky, and harsh trails. She found their features wholly unlike those of the Negro, except where they have cohabited below the ridge in the Black Water Swamp. Dromgoole pictured the pure Melungeons as presenting a characteristic and individual appearance.[9]

It is interesting to study different, more current, writers who quote the descriptions of this particular early writer and state them with subtle, but totally different outcomes. Ms. Dromgoole has been widely read and quoted, with more than one recent writer using her observations with the addition of the words "fine looking" for the men and "soft and lovely" for the descriptions of the women. Apparently, the later writer thought these people handsome and felt it necessary, consciously or unconsciously, to embellish the earlier text. Another writer quoted Dromgoole with the addition of "small" to the earlier description of the typical female hands. Modest, subjective changes such as these lead to historical distortions of the physical description of these people.

Moving into the twentieth century, William S. Pollitzer and William H. Brown of the Department of Anatomy and Department of Anthropology Genetics Training Committee of the University of North Carolina studied a representative sample of the Hancock County Melungeons in 1965. A local physician by the name of Dr. Pierce enabled the researchers to conduct the study by assuring the skeptical Melungeons of potential health benefits from a health survey that was to be strictly a study of their differences from the general white population.

The methodology as described was:

"In 1965, 72 subjects were studied; in 1966, 105 additional subjects were studied. Of the 177 total, 50 were adult males (16 and over), 78 were adult females, and 49 were children (6 through 15). A brief medical history, age, birthplace of subject and of parents, and of kinship information for the construction of a pedigree were obtained. A superficial inspection of eyes and mouth was usually included. On all subjects, blood and urine samples were obtained, and hair form and hair color were observed. Skin color was determined on the medial surface of the upper arm by photometer (Photovolt Model 610), using both red and tristimulus filters, on subjects of the second survey only. Height, weight, face width, face length, nose width, and nose length were measured on adults in both surveys: head length and head width were also measured on adults in the second survey; and appropriate indices were calculated."[10]

Table 3 (next page) showed the subjects of the study to be considerably lighter than Negroes and generally in the color range for white-admixed Catawba Indians studied by Pollitzer in 1967. On the tristimulus scale, with the lower numbers designating darker, Negroes were 11.3, Catawba Indians 35.7, and Melungeons 42.

Table 4 showed the population to be moderately tall with mesocephalic, meso to leptoproscopic, and leptorrine, and thus

Skin color determinations by reflectometry with two filters are shown in Table 3, with sexes and age groups separated. The lower the number, the darker the color. The readings with the tristimulus filter may be

TABLE 3

Skin color in Melungeons *

Age	N	Mean for Males Tristimulus Filter	Red Filter	N	Mean for Females Tristimulus Filter	Red Filter
Below 16	25	39.8	55.4	31	41.0	56.1
16-40	18	40.9	56.4	32	42.8	57.6
Above 40	20	45.2	58.2	29	44.0	57.7

* Readings are measures of light reflectance from the skin, an indication of melanization. Magnesium oxide on this scale is 100%.

TABLE 4

Morphology in adult Melungeons *

	N	Males Mean	Min-Max	S.D.	N	Females Mean	Min-Max	S.D.
Height (cm)	50	170.9	152-188	8.1	78	161.5	137-175	6.4
Weight (kg)	50	69.6	42-119	15.4	77	61.1	42-108	11.8
Head Length (mm)	36	193.0	180-204	6.8	56	186.1	171-206	6.1
Head Breadth (mm)	36	149.9	138-161	5.2	56	146.1	135-155	4.8
Cephalic Index	36	77.7	70-84	3.1	56	78.6	73-85	2.6
Face Length (mm)	50	123.5	106-141	7.9	77	113.0	96-128	6.1
Face Breadth (mm)	50	136.3	125-151	6.2	78	130.9	120-141	5.0
Facial Index	50	89.2	62-100	6.9	77	86.4	73-98	5.1
Nose Length (mm)	50	55.8	44-69	5.0	77	51.1	44-58	3.3
Nose Width (mm)	49	37.1	31-44	3.1	77	33.8	28-40	2.7
Nasal Index	49	67.8	45-87	8.4	77	66.4	48-85	6.8
Skin Color-T	38	43.2	28-52	5.5	61	43.4	30-49	5.3
Skin Color-R	38	57.3	43-63	4.4	61	57.7	46-62	4.1

* Skin color–T is the reading on the Photometer with the tristimulus or amber filter; skin color–R is the reading with the red filter.

compared with 11.3 for Negro males on James Island, S. C., and 35.7 for white-admixed Catawba Indians (Pollitzer et al., 1967). The tend-

Pollitzer Chart. Courtesy of William Pollitzer

within the Caucasoid range.

Pollitzer and Brown observed 182 persons for hair form and hair color. Of the 182, 120 were straight, 55 were wavy to curly, and seven were kinky. The colors were 85 brown, 65 black, and 20 blond. Twelve subjects were gray or white.[11]

The local people did not derive any of the perceived health benefits from the Pollitzer and Brown study. At the conclusion of this anthropological study, they only remembered their expectations of some free medical reports from the doctors in white coats. This non-medical analysis added another chapter to their repertory of mistrust with the outside world.[12]

Even today, groups are studying those called Melungeons to try to isolate distinguishing characteristics that differentiate them from others in their communities. In Western Virginia, a resurgence of interest led by Dr. Brent Kennedy has inspired several new observations. A dentist in Norton, Virginia, has observed a distinctive shovel shape on the back of the teeth of many of the people claiming to be Melungeons. Archaeologists working with Dr. Kennedy have noticed a distinctive cranial bump on the upper rear skull of many of these same people. The studies continue. All observations will be a piece of the puzzle that tries to define the appearance of this isolate of people.[13]

Attempts to define the uniform appearance of the people known as Melungeons may not have been as difficult during their early organizational period as it is today, because they might have had many more distinctive racial differences than their neighbors. Over time, many distinctly identifiable differences have been forgotten or diluted with a surrounding majority. Our present dilemma with physical appearances is a result of too few early records, too many previous subjective observations, and an earlier lack of cooperation by the identifiable people who were rebelling against their alien environments. Neither funds nor interest have been forthcoming to enhance our knowledge through extensive DNA studies.

As the above samples generally insinuate, Melungeons are described as dark-skinned, but not too dark. Perhaps more olive, reddish-brown, or coppery-colored. Eye color seems to range from black to gray, with an occasional blue, and hair, dark brown to black, with even a few blondes. As for features, the noses range from narrow and pointed to classic Greek. Lips are small to slightly predominate. As in many different races, the women are frequently considered attractive by men of lighter color.

We can observe photographs of Melungeons, dating from the late 1800s to the present, for additional visual information of possible distinguishing appearances. These observations assume that the people photographed are distinct representatives of the group in their era and not mixtures resulting from years of blending with other types outside their isolated area.

Susanna "Sookie" Gibson, born 1795 in North Carolina. Courtesy of William Grohse (deceased) Mattie Mae Grohse.

Frank and Docia Collins Miser Frank b.1876-d.1947 - Described as tall and lanky. Probably over 6 feet tall. Docia b. 1868-d.1936- Described as tall and heavy. Courtesy of Helen Mullins (deceased) Billie Mullins Horton.

Gladys Miser with grandson and nephews.- b. 1918. Courtesy of Cecil and Polly Miser.

The photos show a variation of appearances. The first photo of Susanna "Sookie" Gibson, with noticeably high cheekbones and dark features, shows her sitting with her daughter and grand-daughters, who seem to have less pronounced facial features.

In the second illustration, Frank and Docia Miser were large people, with Docia's features being somewhat distorted by her weight, which was estimated to be over three hundred pounds. Docia was described by early Presbyterian missionaries living in the area as fleshy, dark, and strongly showing Indian blood. Both she and Frank were direct descendants of Solomon and Vardy Collins, as were many of the residents of the area in the 1800s.

The last photo was taken in the 1990s, therefore, with more accurate film technology and exposure. Gladys Miser and kin are dark with moderate features. Gladys was always considered a beautiful woman.

[1]Samuel Cole Williams, *Early Travels in the Tennessee Country*, 1540-1800, Johnson City : The Watauga Press, 1928, pp. 24-29.

[2]Ibid., p. 28

[3]Ibid., p. 29

[4]SL Sheperd, *Memoirs of a Judge Lewis Sheperd*, Chattanooga, 1915,p.83

[5]Ibid., pp. 84-88

[6]Ibid., pp. 394-399

[7]Swan M. Burnett, "Notes on the Melungeons," *American Anthropologist*, Vol. II, 1889, p. 348

[8]Ibid., p. 349

[9]Will Allen Dromgoole, " The Malungeons," *The Arena*, Vol. 3, March 1891, Boston, MA, p.476

[10]William S. Pollitzer and William H. Brown, " Survey of Demography, Anthropometry, and Genetics in the Melungeons of Tennessee: An Isolate of Hybrid Origin in Process of Dissolution.." *Human Biology*, Vol. 41, No.3, 1969, p. 393.

[11]Ibid., pp. 394-395

[12]Interviews with Helen Mullins and Hughie and Laura Mullins.

[13]Scott Collins, member of Dr. Brent Kennedy's research team, Sneedville, Tennessee.

Chapter 3
The Phoenicians

A few basic, more viable theories of Melungeon origin are repeated by researchers over and over, and we will examine each of them, with omission of minor, possibly valid, theories. It seems prudent to start searching for the place of origin of these mysterious people at their earliest theoretical establishment and work toward more current times of their settlement in North America.

The earliest possible date for boat people to have reached the American continent has been placed at around 600 B.C. The Phoenicians were a people with such seafaring skill as to conquer the mighty expanse of the Atlantic at an early time.

Just who were the Phoenicians, and what was their culture? It would be informative to take a more in-depth look at the earlier history of these people, as the gaps in chronology and technology cause many historians to be skeptical of their possible seaworthy accomplishments and skills.

The Phoenician civilization first came to prominence in what are now the countries of Lebanon and southern Syria in about 1200 B.C.

The Phoenicians were not evolutionary pioneers in the concept of using the sea for the betterment of their civilization; their predecessors and neighbors, the Minoans, had developed their society from the isle of Crete between 3100-1200 B.C. The two highly civilized people followed each other in the development of navigation and their own respective alphabets. They shared a similar Semitic language and a nautical way of life. In this early historical period, people did not share the seas and compete fairly, even though they were compatible in many ways. Trade was decided only occasionally by alliances, more often by war, or frequently by a decline in resources of a major power. The Minoans weakened on the Isle of Crete and lost control of the Aegean forever. Their eventual disappearance as a power left the seas to the Phoenicians.

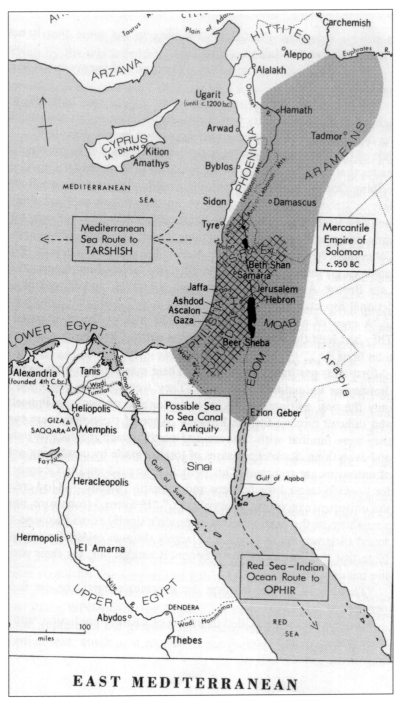

EAST MEDITERRANEAN

Map of Early Phoenicia. Courtesy of Crown Publishers.

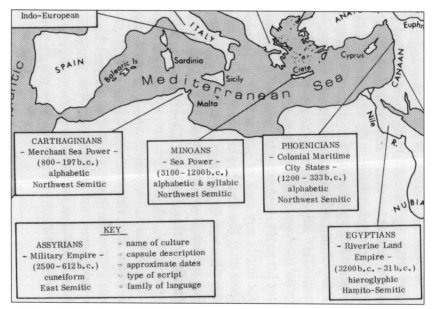

Map of Minoa. Ibid.

The Phoenicians were rich in tradeable items. They manufactured transparent glass, metal objects, and purple dyes from sea mollusks. Their mollusk dye was unique and so expensive that it became the preferred color of royalty throughout their known world.[1] They also traded the gold and silver of Africa, the copper of Cyprus, the ivory of India, and the tin and lead of Spain.[2]

So why would we look at the Phoenicians as possible world explorers and early colonizers of remote places such as the hills of East Tennessee? The Phoenicians were an advanced civilization that spread trade and culture around the known world of their time. As early as 814 B.C., they had built the modern city of Carthage on the distant North African coast. Their empire was extensive for the period, nearly a century before the mighty Romans built a small village that became Rome.

Let us take a look at their unique sailing skills and conquests. Herodotus told of Pharaoh Necho of Egypt commissioning the Phoenicians to sail from their cities of Tyre and Sidon on the Mediterranean through the Red Sea and around Africa in 600 B.C. (page 22). Such a trip took up to three years, and Herodotus told in detail why the voyage took so long to complete. The sailors had to

Map of Phoenician Empire and Carthage, 814 B.C. Courtesy of National Geographic Society

stop more than once to plant, grow, and harvest food for the voyage. Herodotus eventually disputed their overall success. The voyagers reported the sun on their right as they sailed west past the Cape of Good Hope. Later scholars read the writings of Herodotus to understand the Phoenicians had sailed south beyond the Tropic of Capricorn where the sun crosses the sky in the north to the right

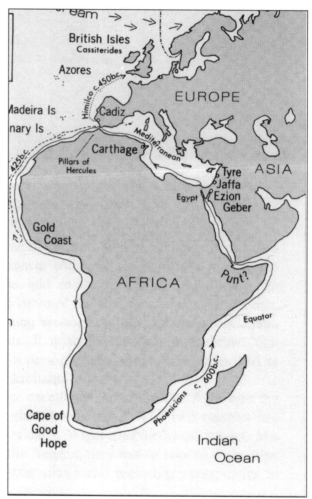

Map of Phoenician Ships around Africa 600 B.C. Ibid.

of the ships heading west.[3]

Many scholars feel these mighty seamen with a Hebrew religion and Oriental culture continued to develop their sea empire with frequent passages out beyond Gibraltar to the British Isles, the Baltics, and beyond. Dr. Cyrus H. Gordon, a leading educator of Mediterranean studies at Brandeis University, translated a stone found in Brazil in 1892 to read: ten Phoenician ships left an island in the Gulf of Aquaba, sailed down the Red Sea, and around Africa. One of the ten ships was separated by a storm and apparently caught the west-flowing South Equatorial Currents to South America. This translation was dated in the 6th century B.C.[4]

Another story of this period told of a Phoenician ship, the *Phoenix*, appropriately decorated with the head of a large bird carved on its bow, landing in South Carolina around 600 B.C. It was theorized that these people were not anxious to conquer and exploit the Native Americans; therefore, they were accepted and thrived 2,000 years before Columbus.[5] Perhaps their darker skin was another survival benefit?

Skeptics wonder how these people could have conquered the mighty Atlantic when most of the people in their time thought the sea ended at Gibraltar. It is written that their ships were much larger than later ships, such as the *Nina, Pinta,* and *Santa Marie,* a fact which would be a benefit to survival. How could their ships be larger than those of the 15th century? The answer lies in the reason for their wealth and power. They were solely dependent upon the control of the sea for their economy. Later, the Romans were a land and continental economy. Gradually, their need or knowledge for building larger ships diminished as land-based segments of the Roman civilization flourished. Ships were slow to evolve in size after the long period of the land-based Roman Empire.

Another facet to consider in the examination of the Phoenician period was a unique map. The map was called *Piri Reis* after a Turkish man named Pira who was an admiral or chief (translated as *Reis*). This parchment map was rediscovered in Istanbul in 1929 and was dated 1513. Piri Reis wrote that the map was from an ancient source and period. It has been theorized that the map was from the library at Alexandria, which was destroyed in the seventh century A.D. This historical map shows the correct coastline of Antarctica that has been covered by ice since 4000 B.C. and has only been defined in the last 30 years by soundings. This map shows the coast of Africa and the eastern part of the Amazon with considerable accuracy.[6] The longitude of South America is correct in its relationship with the Old World. Many of the rivers of South America are also illustrated in their correct perspective.[7]

The resource materials seem to point to a highly sophisticated nation of Phoenicians who ruled the seas prior to the Roman Empire. Their capital city of Tyre in the eastern Mediterranean

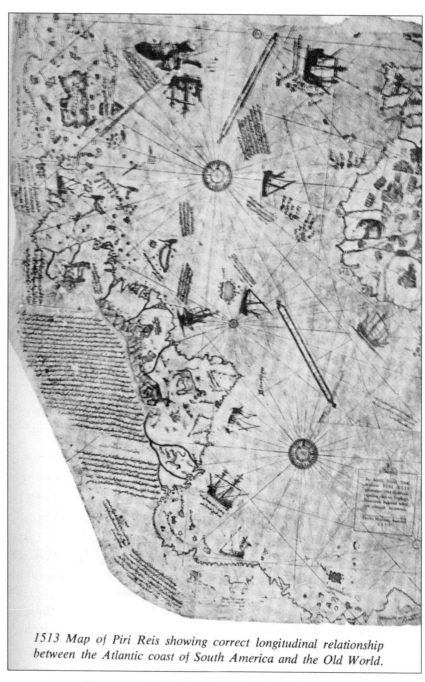

1513 Map of Piri Reis showing correct longitudinal relationship between the Atlantic coast of South America and the Old World.

Piri Reis Map. Courtesy of Chilton Book Company

Proof of validity of Piri Reis. Letter of Lt. Colonel Ohlmeyer USAF[8].
Courtesy of Chilton Book Company.

eventually lost importance and status to their colony at Carthage on
the north coast of Africa. The Phoenicians then ruled the seas from
Carthage until they were defeated by the Romans in 146 B.C. Their
city was razed and destroyed, and they never regained prominence
in world affairs. Historians theorized that the remnant people of
their once mighty civilization ended up in Morocco, the Iberian
Peninsula, or fled to other distant havens. Some of their supposed
distant ports of refuge will be examined later in the text, with their
descendants being possible ancestors of the Melungeons.

Before we leave these ancient people, it is pertinent to check
archaeological evidence in the Americas for any sign that they may
have visited the distant shores. In Central America, this incense

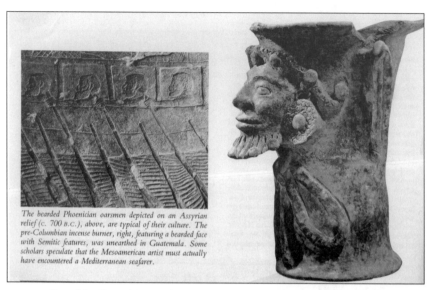

The bearded Phoenician oarsmen depicted on an Assyrian relief (c. 700 B.C.), above, are typical of their culture. The pre-Columbian incense burner, right, featuring a bearded face with Semitic features, was unearthed in Guatemala. Some scholars speculate that the Mesoamerican artist must actually have encountered a Mediterranean seafarer.

Possible Phoenician influence. Courtesy of the British Museum.

burner was found (above). The burner is compared to the faces on an Assyrian relief of 600 B.C. Notice the similar facial features of the two objects.

Closer to the subjects of our inquiry, an engraved Phoenician tablet was found at the base of Mammoth Mound in Moundsville, West Virginia, in 1838 (next page). At the time, the tablet could not be deciphered, but scholars attributed the mound to very early European visitors (pre-1492). The hypothesis was accepted for the next forty years, before the early historians fueled the eventual widespread beliefs that Columbus was the first European discoverer. Over time, the Moundsville tablet was forgotten, considered Cherokee by some, and only a misplaced artifact by others. In 1968, an epigrapher by the name of Diringer brought the tablet forth for renewed and further study. Controversy still surrounds the exact translation, but the stone is believed to be Punic inscription (Phoenician), used during the first century B.C.[9]

Another striking Phoenician example from a North American Mound Builder burial mound is illustrated on page 28. On the left is a terra-cotta head excavated in North America. The head has the typical Phoenician hat and is dated to 6th Century B.C. The similiar head on the right is of the same period and is from Hogia Irene,

Examples of Iberian inscriptions from North America (left), and from Europe (right). The American inscription, engraved on a stone tablet, was found in 1838 at a depth of 60 feet in a large burial mound at Grave Creek, West Virginia, together with a skeleton and copper arm rings. It was at once recognized by Professor Rafn of Copenhagen as being Iberian, though that script had not at that time been deciphered. Recent studies show that the language of the tablet is Punic (Phoenician), written in the form of alphabet used in Spain during the first millennium B.C. It may be translated as follows (the writing reading from right to left):

(1) The mound raised-on-high for Tasach
(2) This tile
(3) (His) queen caused-to-be-made

The alphabet of the tablet was deciphered by Spanish scholars, and published by the English epigrapher D. Diringer in 1968. The language is basic Semitic, and all words occur in standard literary Semitic dictionaries, such as that of Professor Wehr. The decipherment of the tablet is explained by Fell in *Occasional Publications*, vol. 3, issued by the Epigraphic Society.

The European inscription, with which scholars such as Rafn and Schoolcraft compared the Grave Creek inscription, and shown to the right of the Grave Creek tablet, is written in the Iberian alphabet and in the Punic language, but alternate lines read from right to left, and then from left to right (this is called *boustrophedon*, meaning "as a plowman walks"). The translation, by Fell, is as follows:

(1) Various ways of making a prediction
(2) The planets reveal indications of . . . (letters missing)
(3) He who understands how, may himself obtain information about hidden truths
(4) When the radiant gleam is seen of the myriads of the heavenly host following their courses on high
(5) The directions of their wanderings are the signs of omens
(6) The crescent moon, appearing below the planet Mars, is a favorable sign
(7) When Venus makes a transit through the constellation of the Ram
(8) She bestows upon mankind peace and mild government

The tablet, evidently only the first part of an astrological text, is deciphered in detail in the *Occasional Publications*, vol. 3, of the Epigraphic Society.

Moundsville Tablet. Courtesy of Barry Fell.

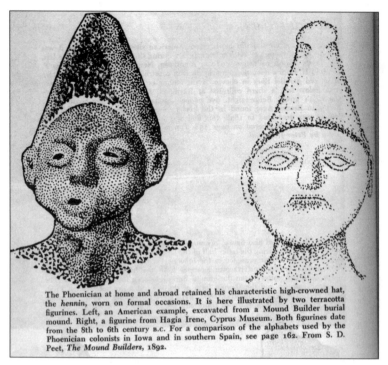

The Phoenician at home and abroad retained his characteristic high-crowned hat, the *hennin*, worn on formal occasions. It is here illustrated by two terracotta figurines. Left, an American example, excavated from a Mound Builder burial mound. Right, a figurine from Hagia Irene, Cyprus Museum. Both figurines date from the 8th to 6th century B.C. For a comparison of the alphabets used by the Phoenician colonists in Iowa and in southern Spain, see page 162. From S. D. Peet, *The Mound Builders*, 1892.

Phoenician with Hennin Hat. Courtesy of Barry Fell

Cyprus Museum.

Also of interest to our investigation, several ancient coins have been found and documented on a farm in Blackwater, Virginia. A person living in Rogersville, Tennessee, is credited with owning a Lydian coin, a Greek coin, and several other coins found by his grandfather.[10] The Greek coin, with Alexander the Great on one side and Zeus on the other was available to photograph and identify.

Any discrepancy of time period can be justified by understanding that the Phoenician period was 1200 B.C.-64 B.C. the Lydian 600 B.C.-546 B.C. and that of Alexander, 336 B.C.-323 B.C. The Phoenicians were conquered in sequence by the Neo-Babylonians, Egyptians, Persians, Alexander, and finally ceased to exist as a separate entity in 64 B.C., becoming a part of the Roman portion of Syria. All during these periods, the separate peoples interchanged ideas, trade, goods, monies, and utilized Phoenician sailing expertise to broaden their exposure to the known world.

What is the significance of the coins? Who were the Lydians?

Ancient Coins. Courtesy of Britannica

The Lydians lived in Asia Minor, just north of Phoenicia, and were credited, along with the Ionian Greeks, as being one of the earliest producers of money. The date of their earliest known coinage was around 600 B.C. Production continued in Lydia for several hundred years and constituted the chief currency of the Near Eastern world. A vast amount of these types of coins were distributed during the period.

The Greek coin found in Blackwater, Tennessee, would have been of a later date, but it should not be discounted as evidence. Rome destroyed Carthage in 146 B.C.; at this later date, the Carthaginians were dispersed and might have carried Greek coins to their new destination.

Consider the Phoenicians' capablility of crossing the seas, their possible physical appearance, artifacts found in North America representing their earlier presence, and be prepared to move forward into history to examine other origin theories of the mysterious Melungeons.

[1]Charles Michael Boland, *They All Discovered America,* Random House, Inc., New York, 1961
[2]Byron Longman, *Who Really Discovered the New World?*, Duskin/McGraw-Hill, 1979, pp. 51-60
[3]Cyrus H.Gordon, *Before Columbus.* New York, Crown Publishers, Inc., 1971, p. 149
[4] *Mysteries of the Ancient Americas*, Reader's Digest Association, Inc., Pleasantville, New York, 1986, p. 18
[5]James Ewing, *The Tennessee Conservationist,* Volume XXXV, July 1970.
[6]Cyrus H. Gordon, *Before Columbus,* New York, Crown Publishers, Inc. 1971, pp. 70,106.
[7]ibid
[8]Graham Hancock, *Fingerprints of the Gods,* New York, Crown Publishers, Inc., 1995, p. 3.
[9]Barry Fell, *America B.C.,* Pocket Books, 1989, New York, pp. 21, 156.
[10]Rollin W. Gillespie, *A Theory Considering the Melungeons,* Bellingham, Washington, 1989.

Chapter 4
The Lost Tribe

The second theory of Melungeon origin relates to a time when one of the tribes of the Bible might have migrated from the turmoil of governmental unrest to a new land. The original report of displacement began after the reign and death of Solomon in 915 B.C. Solomon was replaced by his son, Rehoboam, who lost the cohesiveness of the United Kingdom. The eventual split became known as Judah to the south and Israel to the north.

This event produced a revolutionary named Jeroboam. He had fled to exile in Egypt, only to return to Israel and lead a revolt against Rehoboam, who refused to reduce taxes. Subsequently, the ten tribes of the Northern kingdom chose Jeroboam as king and named their country Israel. The remaining two tribes of Israel, Benjamin and Judah, formed the Southern tribe that they named Judah.[1]

The Northern Kingdom of Israel lasted 200 years before it was conquered by Assyria in 721 B.C. Their capital of Samaria was destroyed, and the people were deported or they disappeared. The fate of the ten tribes of the Northern kingdom was lost to speculation, but theories have revived that their ultimate settlement was in various faraway lands. Tradition speaks of these people, although incorrectly, as the Ten Lost Tribes.[2] The Southern Kingdom of Judah was destroyed by Babylon in 586 B.C. Many of the people of these tribes were carried to exile in Babylonia, while others fled to Egypt.[3] People of the Ten Lost Tribes are later referred to as a historical linkage to Melungeons.

Jewish history continued in quite a tumultuous fashion after this period, and the people of the area were constantly in a state of flux and dissolution. The Egyptians, Greeks, and Romans all controlled the country for a period of time.

Many centuries later, the Roman emperor Hadrian undertook to rebuild Jerusalem as a new and pagan city, which led to a rebellion in 132-135 A.D. by Bar Kochba.⁴ This later chaotic period, and Bar Kochba, will be linked to archaeological findings in Melungeon areas. Let us use this information to explore the possibility of the Lost Tribes or some remnant of Semitic people being on the American continent before other peoples from across the seas. As we consider these people, we must also remember their close proximity to the Phoenicians with their Semitic language, who lived just north of present-day Israel.

Much later in history, Jewish cultural influences began to be reported in distant places. In 1650, a rabbi, Manasseh ben Israel from Amsterdam, traveling near Quito, Equador, reported being greeted by natives with "Shelma Israel (Hear, O Israel)." It was reported that many people of the same origin were living in the highlands around Quito. The rabbi reported his findings to Oliver Cromwell in London in order to prove the prophesy that the Messiah would return for the second time, once Jews were scattered throughout the world. The rabbi's motive was to gain acceptance of Jews into England; his story did not convince Cromwell.⁵

James Adair, who traded among the Indians for 40 years, wrote

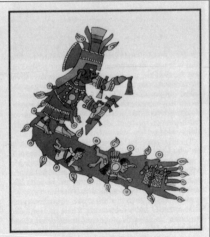

Lord Kingsborough was convinced that the Indians of Mexico were directly descended from Israel's Ten Lost Tribes. As proof, he spent his fortune on reproducing volumes of Aztec codices that, he claimed, illustrated biblical events. The two reproduced here are said to represent the story of Adam and Eve, left, and a primordial deluge, above.

Left- Adam & Eve. Right- The Flood. Courtesy of Rare Books Division, New York Public Library, Astor, Lenox & Tilden Foundation.

a book in the 1700s comparing them to Jews. He reported hearing the word "Jehovah" in their chants. Their word for dead or lost was "Illeht Kancha," meaning "gone to Canaan." He reported the Indians met at night to revitalize their spirits to Yohewah as they sang the Hebrew word for the Messiah.[6]

Moving up toward North America in the 1800s, Edward King (Lord Kingsborough), a member of Parliament, attempted to tie the Indians of Mexico to the Lost Tribe. King spent his fortune and lifetime trying to publish his studies of people who he believed were descendants of the Lost Tribe. Much of his authority was taken from James Adair. He never accomplished his goals, as he was thrown in debtor's prison twice for failure to pay publishing costs. In 1837, he was imprisoned for the third time, where he subsequently died at age 42. The photographs on page 31 of Indian pictures intrepreted as Adam and Eve and the Flood are examples of his theories.[7]

George Catlin, an American artist, traveled extensively among remote tribes of North America from 1832-1839. His paintings and notes are some of the best examples of Native American appearances and customs prior to the European influences. This headdress (page 33) painted by Catlin was described as resembling that of the regalia of Old Testament Hebrews.[8]

At about the same time, the Church of Jesus Christ of Latter-Day Saints published a revelation by Joseph Smith. It was reported that in 1830, Smith received some sacred golden plates from the angel Moroni in New York State. The plates did not specifically mention one of the Lost Tribes of Israel, but referred to Jews known as Jaredites fleeing to America after their failed attempt to build the Tower of Babel. It is theorized the first group fled to America and settled in Mexico or further south. The Jaredites prospered, but according to tradition, once again forgot their Lord and were destroyed around 600 B.C.

After the collapse of the Jaredites, followers of the prophet Lehi landed in Mesoamerica and immediately split into two factions. The Neophytes became the ruling tribe and strengthened themselves by joining some descendants of the southern tribes of Judah. They prospered and built many of the pre-Columbian cities of Mesoamerica.

The Author painting a Chief at the base of the Rocky Mountains.

G. Catlin.

George Catlin Painting Chief Four Bears. Courtesy of Dover Publishing.

A tribe called the Laminites became their rival ruling tribe. They were thought to have wandered to the Americas some time during the first millennium B.C. Some even theorize the Lamanite's civilization progressed upward, and, eventually, they became the mound-building Indians of Ohio.[9]

The Mormons accept these tenets as a history of their faith. They place the second appearance of Christ among their Indian ancestors in Mexico. He is believed to have appeared before over three thousand Indians. The myths of white, bearded, God-like rulers among the great Indian civilizations of the Americas is given by the Mormans as additional proof of the appearance of Christ in America.[10]

A Morman writer attributes the migratory success of the Mormons to their belief in the voyages of the Laminites, who were absorbed into the Native American population. Many Indians called the Mormons "Americrats" and trusted them above all other whites.[11]

Like the earlier Jaredites who continually forgot their God, the Jewish tribes of the Laminites and Nephites carried on the fallen tradition. Several times God punished them with natural catastrophes. At one point, the resurrected Christ was sent to save the Nephites. Nothing succeeded with the decadent Nephites, and they were annihilated on a narrow peninsula in their own territory. The golden plates delivered to Joseph Smith in New York by the angel Moroni were proof of this Jewish ancestry. [12]

Closer to the target area of the Melungeons we find another tribe with many activities relating to the Old Testament. The Yuchi tribe appears in many mysteries of the early settlement of the North American continent as well as those of early Melungeons. They lived in the correct area, with their earliest known location in East-

Angel Moroni. Courtesy of Granger Collection of New York

ern Tennessee near present-day Manchester. Some were known to be further east, while others were reported as far west as Muscle Shoals, Alabama.

Dr. Joseph B. Mahan, Jr., Director of Education and Research at the Columbus (Georgia) Museum of Arts and Crafts in the 1960s, was an expert on American Indian ethnology and archaeology who specialized in the Yuchi tribe. He reported the following similarities between Hebrew and Yuchi celebrations: Both celebrate (1) an eight-day festival that starts (2) on the fifteenth day (or full moon) of the holy harvest month. Throughout this holiday, (3) they live in booths (4) at a cultic center where (5) they nurture a sacred fire. To this day, the Jews follow the first three items. They have dropped number four as they are now dispersed throughout the world and do not have a cultic center. Number five has been dropped because sacrifices have not been performed since the loss of the Second Temple in 70 A.D.

Both groups make circumambulations on their respective festivals. The Yuchi circle was a fire in the sacred cultic area with a large, foliage-crested branch. The Jews shake a combination of plants lashed together on the Festival of Tabernacles.[13]

A stone was found in the Yuchi area in 1966 by Manfred Metcalf; therefore, the stone was named the Metcalf Stone (see page 36). Numerous authorities such as Mahan and Cyrus Gordon attempted translation of the mysterious stone. The scholars surmised the stone to be of Near Eastern origins. The script seemed to be Aegean with a Phoenician influence.[14] The world is still waiting for the knowledge to confirm the translations of this historical object.

Mahan and Gordon both concluded that the Yuchis were not one of the Ten Lost Tribes, but that they shared certain cultural features with the early Hebrews. They feel both had cultural roots in an Eastern Mediterannean civilization of the Bronze Age.

The object that seems to have more acceptance to the Lost Tribe theory is the Bat Creek Stone (see pages 37 and 38). This inscribed stone was found in Loudon County, Tennessee, in the late 1800s. Excavations were made on a mound 28 feet in diameter and five feet high. Near the bottom of the mound, nine skeletons were found. Seven individuals were buried side by side with skulls facing north, and the other two were separated, with one skull facing

Metcalf Stone. Courtesy of Crown Publishing.

north and the other south. Relics were found only by the skeleton facing to the north. Under the skull and jawbone were found two copper bracelets, an inscribed stone, a drilled fossil, a copper bead, a bone implement, and small pieces of polished wood.[15]

The Bat Creek Stone was housed in the Smithsonian Institute and made little impression on professional archaeologists because it had been found by an amateur. At the time of discovery in 1890-1891, it was read upside down and reported to be Cherokee script.

The stone was reexamined by Dr. Joseph B. Mahan, Jr. He read the stone inscription as Canaanite. He was priviledged to use a very clear photograph of the original stone, which enhanced the script for better clarity. He translated the stone to read "Year 1 of the

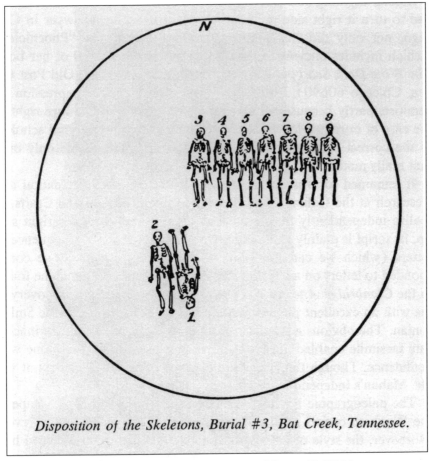

Disposition of the Skeletons, Burial #3, Bat Creek, Tennessee.

Bat Creek Burial Mound. Courtesy of Crown Publishing

Golden Age for the Jew." Some problems were encountered with the exact reading of every letter, but the letter-forms seem to represent a time of 100 A.D. The Jews fled the Romans during the First (66-70 A.D.) or Second (132-135 A.D.) rebellions.[16]

The translation of the Bat Creek Stone can be identified more accurately when tied to coins excavated in Louisville, Hopkinsville, and Clay City, Kentucky. These are Hebrew coins of Bar Kokhba's rebellion against Rome in 132-135 A D. One coin shows the name of Simon, which was Bar Kohba's personal name. The other side reads "Year 2 of the Freedom of Israel" (i. e. 133 A.D.). The coins made little impression on historians at the time, perhaps because, again, they were found by nonprofessionals.[17]

Bat Creek Stone. Excavated in Loudon County, Tennessee, during the Smithsonian Mound Exploration Program under the direction of Professor Cyrus Thomas and the field supervision of J. W. Emmert. Discovered in 1885 and accessioned into the Museum in 1889. *Courtesy, The Smithsonian Institution, Department of Anthropology.*

Bat Creek Stone. Courtesy of The Smithsonian Institution, Department of Anthropology

Bar Kokhba Coins

Bar Kokhba Coins

Bar Kokhba Coins.

Bar Kokhba Coins. Courtesy of Crown Publishing

The finding of the Bar Kokhba Coins in relation to the Bat Creek Stone implies Jewish refugees fled to the North American continent around 135 A.D., even though ethnic cleansing had occurred in their area since 600-700 B.C.

Despite the lack of professional interest in these complimentary finds, it seems illogical to believe the Bat Creek tomb is of Cherokee origin, with the inscribed stone being a relic obtained by a member of a Native American tribe sometime after 1492. This false logic would have had the stone buried with the deceased in eternal memory of Eastern Mediterranean archaeology.

If we accept the hypothesis of the Bat Creek Stone, the Bar Kokhba Coins, the Metcalf Stone, and the dogma of the Church of Jesus Christ of the Latter-Day Saints, the Jews were wandering around the southeastern United States a little less than 2000 years ago. Intermarriage and cultural exchange with Native Americans would have been possible. Another positive factor was the earlier examples of known Semitic or Asiatic words being used by various tribes. Samuel Morrison tells stories of Hebrew-speaking Indians, first by Spanish explorers and, particularly, by English Puritans, who toyed with the idea that the American aborigines were one of the Lost Tribes of Israel. Thomas Throwgood, in *Jews in America* (London, 1650), claimed to have heard the Indians of New England use the word 'Hallelujah!'"[18]

To explain the evidence as anything other than Jews making contact with America around 200 A.D. can only amount to scholarly denial, arrogance, and ignorance of our past. The excavations attest inscriptionally and archaeologically to a migration from Israel to our Southeast. Were these the first arrivals of the mysterious Melungeons or just another dark-skinned group absorbed in our mysterious past?

---

[1]Henry H. Halley, *Halley's Bible Handbook*, Zondervan Publishing House, 1927,Grand Rapids, Michigan, p. 193.

[2]*The Lincoln Library of Essential Information*, Frontier Press Company, 1947, Buffalo, New York, p. 492.

[3]ibid

[4]William T. Couch, *Collier's Encyclopedia*, P.F. Collier and Son, 1955,New York, Volume 11, pp. 386-387.

[5]*Mysteries Of The Ancient Americas*, Reader's Digest Association, Inc., 1986, Pleasantville, New York, p. 36.

[6]ibid

[7]ibid

[8]George Catlin, *North American Indians*, Dover Publications, Inc. 1973, New York, Volume 1.

[9]Harold Driver, *The Americas on the Eve of Discovery*, New Jersey, Prentice-Hall, 1964, p. 173.

[10]ibid

[11]Robert Mullen, *The Latter-Day Saints: The Mormons Yesterday and Today*, New York, Doubleday, 1966, p. 97.

[12]Mysteries Of The Ancient Americas, Reader's Digest Association, Inc., 1986, Pleasantville, New York, pp. 40-41.

[13]Cyrus H. Gordon, *Before Columbus*, Crown Publishers, Inc., 1971, New York, pp. 89-90.

[14]ibid

[15]ibid p. 179

[16]ibid p. 182-185

[17]ibid p. 175

[18]Samuel Eliot Morison, *The European Discovery of America*, Volume 1, New York, Oxford University Press, 1971, pp. 106-107

Chapter 5
Madoc, Mandans, and Welsh Indians

MADOC I am the sonne of Owain Gwynedd
With stature large, and comely grace adorned:
No lands at home nor store of wealth me please,
My minde was whole to search the Ocean seas.

Hakluyt's Navigations and Discoveries, 1589

Now we jump to 1140 A.D. to visit the enjoyable theory of Prince Madoc of Wales and his crew being the origional Melungeons in America.

The Prince.
Courtesy of Falls of the
Ohio Museum.

The Welsh of this period, and for several hundred years before, were a feudal kingdom constantly at war. Originally Celtic (Romans called them Gauls), they bleached their hair, wore jewelry, and wore bright tunics and chain mail in battle. The Celts strutted before their foes, brandished their arms, boasted, and added insults and challenges to all adversaries. Some warriors were six feet, five inches tall. Even their women were known to have fought and led in battle. The Greek historian Strabo commented, "The whole race is madly fond of war." Their battles were blood-curdling to the blare of boar-headed trumpets, chariots, frantic horses, and screams of the vanquished. They paraded after battles with heads hanging as trophies on their horses while singing in triumph. Later, they embalmed human parts in cedar oil for display of their prowess to all.

In 390 B.C., they sacked Rome, and by 279 B.C., they were recorded to have pillaged the Greek sanctuary of Delphi. In 60 B.C., the Celts were at battle with the Romans in Britain. Led by

Boudicca, Queen of the Iceni, they amassed 230,000 warriors and shattered the Roman forces. The city of Roman London was burned to the ground.

For over 200 years, the Romans occupied Britain but struggled with the people of North Wales. These were the heroic, free-spirited descendants of the Celtic race who later evolved into the Welsh.

A Welsh historian, Giraldus Cambrensis (1147-1223), added more to the perception we have of the Welsh of the period. He described them as "light and active, hardy rather than strong; the nation is universally trained to arms. Meat is consumed by the people more than bread. They fish in little wicker boats or coracles, (page 46 and note for later) which they carry to their rivers.

"They are always ready for war. Lightly armed with small breastplates, helmets, and shields, they attack their mailed foes with lance and arrow. The Celts had some cavalry, but the marshy nature of the soil compelled greater numbers to fight on foot. Abstemious both in food and drink, frugal, and capable of bearing great privations, they watch their enemies through the cold and

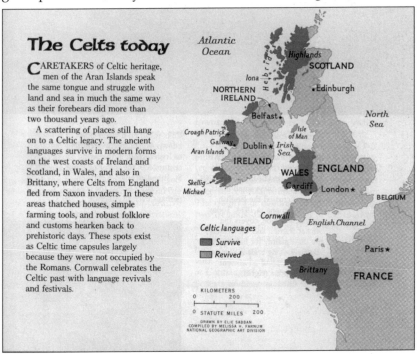

The Celts today

CARETAKERS of Celtic heritage, men of the Aran Islands speak the same tongue and struggle with land and sea in much the same way as their forebears did more than two thousand years ago.

A scattering of places still hang on to a Celtic legacy. The ancient languages survive in modern forms on the west coasts of Ireland and Scotland, in Wales, and also in Brittany, where Celts from England fled from Saxon invaders. In these areas thatched houses, simple farming tools, and robust folklore and customs hearken back to prehistoric days. These spots exist as Celtic time capsules largely because they were not occupied by the Romans. Cornwall celebrates the Celtic past with language revivals and festivals.

Celtic Survivors. Courtesy of National Geographic.

Keeping tradition afloat, Welshman Bernard Thomas navigates the River Teifi in his tub-shaped coracle, a kind of boat Celts paddled. Among the last to make these small boats, Thomas crossed the English Channel in one in 1974. Today canvas, not hide, covers the wicker frames, and the vessels are used mainly for fishing. A similar-looking craft is seen in a plaster copy of an ancient Celtic figurine (**right**).

For ambitious ventures, the Celts relied on a larger boat known as a curragh. According to Irish legend, in the sixth century A.D. the seafaring monk St. Brendan sailed a curragh to new lands across the ocean, perhaps even to America.

Celtic Coracle. Courtesy of National Geographic

stormy nights, always bent upon defense or plunder.

"The heads of families think it is their duty to amuse their guests by their fractiousness. The highest, as well as the lowest of the people, have a remarkable boldness and confidence in speaking and answering, and their natural warmth of temper is distinguished from the English coldness of disposition. They revenge with vehemence any injuries which may tend to the disgrace of their blood, whether an ancient or a recent affront."

Giraldus adds, "They are inconstant, and regardless of any covenant. They commit acts of plunder, not only against foreigners, and hostile nations, but against their own countrymen. Bold in their warlike onsets, they cannot bear a repulse, and trust to flight for safety; but defeated one day, they are ready to resume the conflict on the next. Their ancient national custom of dividing property amongst all the brothers of a house leads to perpetual contests for possessions, and frequent fratricides."[1]

This was the heritage of Madoc and his people. It is important to touch upon the specific chronology and the immediate family of Prince Madoc in order to review the possibility that he sailed toward and reached the American continent.

The family lineage is recorded in Welsh history, but we will begin with Owain Gwynedd, the father of Prince Madoc. Owain succeeded his father in 1137 A.D. One of his parents was of Viking extraction, of which it is said that some were dark-skinned citizens. Owain fought in many battles with Irish, Normans, French, and Flemings, and he even fought his own brother, Cadwaladr.

In 1157, King Henry II of England attacked Owain Gwynedd and was repulsed. Henry withdrew from battle, and afterward, many called Owain "King of Wales." Owain relished his new role and ruled the Welsh with prosperity for all. King Henry II wrote to the Emperor of Constantinople that "there is a people called Welsh, so bold and ferocious that, when unarmed they do not fear to encounter an armed force; being ready to shed their blood for their country and to sacrifice their lives for renown."

Owain Gwynedd had seventeen known sons and two daughters born of two wives. His first wife, Gwaldys, died in 1162, and he married Chrisiant, a first cousin. His second marriage caused considerable disunity in the country as well as in the Catholic Church.

Thomas Beckett, later the Archbishop of Canterbury, excommunicated Owain from the church, but his relationship was accepted by most outside the clergy in the old Celtic tradition.

Madoc was one of nineteen children born of Prince Owain Gwynedd of Wales. There were listed seventeen sons: Rhodri, Cynoric, Riryd, Meredydd, Edwal, Cynan Rein, Maelgon, Llewelyn, Iorweth, Daffydd, Cadwallon, Howell, Cadell, Madoc, Enion, and Philip. The two daughters born were Anagarad, and Gwynllian. Owain fathered many other illegitimate children during his lifetime, and various complications arose among the children over who would eventually inherit the power and wealth of their father. Some say Madoc was one of the illegitimate offspring.

Owain died in 1169, and the factions began to struggle for his power and wealth. His son, Howell, claimed the throne, and while in Ireland to claim his deceased mother's properties, brother Daffydd took control of the Welsh. King Henry II of Britain entered the scheme by offering his sister as a bride to Daffydd. Howell returned only to be slain in an uprising by the people. Eventually Daffydd slew brother Iowerth, imprisoned brother Rhodri, and drove the other brothers into exile. Many feel these events prompted brother Madoc to flee with a fleet of ships across the seas.

A Welsh friend of the author, Mrs. Myfanny Richards, who now lives in Bloomington, Indiana, told of singing an opening tribute each morning in her Welsh primary school to Prince Madoc who sailed the seas to America. This patriotic singing event occurred each and every morning to begin the school day, just as in America we have repeated the Pledge of Allegiance to the flag to start the school day.

The supposed sailing route of Madoc was little different than those of early mariners who reached America. He sailed south to the Canaries or Azores, picked up water and additional provisions, and followed the currents to land somewhere between Central America and the southern part of the North American continent.

A monument stands in Mobile Bay, Alabama, marking the proximity of his initial landing in America. The monument was erected by the Daughters of the American Revolution in 1953. It has this inscription: "In memory of Prince Madoc, a Welsh explorer, who landed on the shores of Mobile Bay in 1170 and left behind, with the

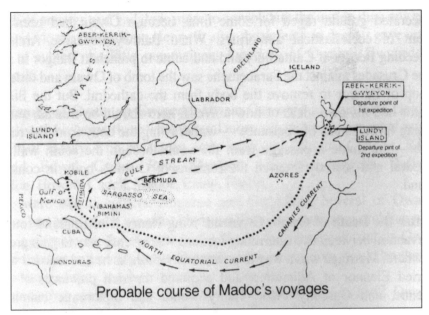

Madoc's Voyages. Courtesy of Dana Olson.

Indians, the Welsh language."[2]

After landing in Mobile Bay on a second voyage, theory has it that over a period of several hundred years the Welsh survived,

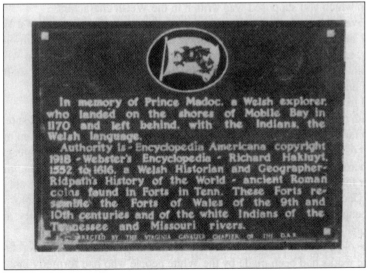

Madoc Monument. Courtesy of Dana Olson.

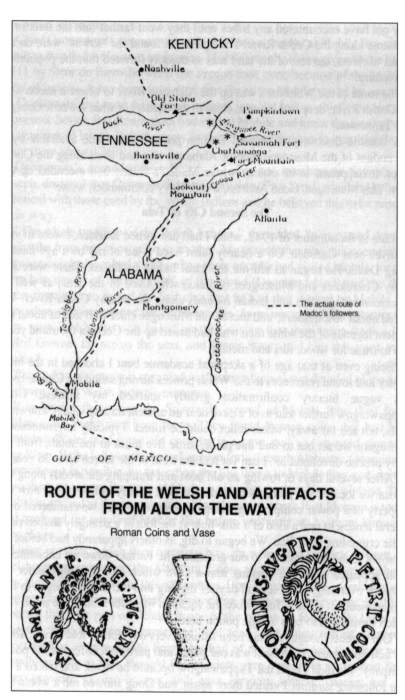

ROUTE OF THE WELSH AND ARTIFACTS FROM ALONG THE WAY

Roman Coins and Vase

Madoc Route. Courtesy of Dana Olson.

multiplied, and followed the rivers northward. They were thought to have settled at several different sites, resulting in progeny dispersed over a large area.

The Old Stone Fort near Manchester, Tennessee, is such a site. This enclosure of fifty acres had walls continuously running a total of 4,600 feet. The construction was originally planned in conjunction with the Bark Camp Fork and the Barren Fork of the Duck River. The steep cliffs were natural barriers for a large portion of the enclosure.

This structure was studied during the settlement of the continent, through the 19th century and into the 20th century, with lit-

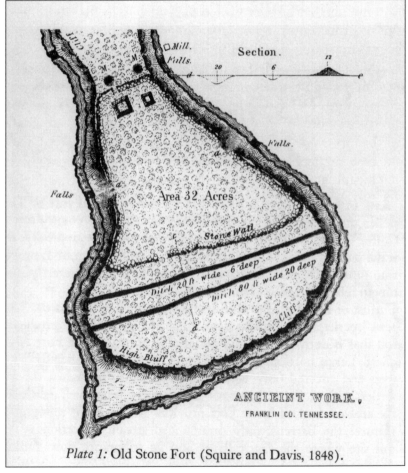

Plate 1: Old Stone Fort (Squire and Davis, 1848).

Old Stone Fort. Courtesy of Charles H. Faulkner.

tle conclusions as to its builders or purposes. John Sevier inquired about the fort while confronting the Cherokee. Sevier questioned Oconostota, the Cherokee war leader, about his knowledge of a white race preceding the Cherokee that built the stone and earthen structure. It is reported that Oconostota responded with a story that pleased Sevier.[3] Other Native Americans carried similar oral beliefs of a white race preceding them to the Southeastern area of the continent, according to Zella Armstong, a Chattanooga writer and historian. She also reinforced the Madoc story by theorizing probable routes from Mobile Bay to East Tennessee.[4]

In 1823, a researcher named Haywood concluded the age of the fort using a tree growing in the wall with 357 rings (years). It is uncertain whether he ever visited the site, but, in 1848, Squire and Davis recorded information very similar to that of C. F. Rafinesque, who was first published in 1819. Squire and Davis had never visited the site. This entire period of the study was based on one observation, and the copycat researchers who followed were not considered as thorough.[5] The questions in this case were if scientific procedures were followed, and when did the tree start growing after the fort was built?

In 1966, archaeologists from the University of Tennessee excavated the fort area and attempted to provide at least partial answers to the puzzling questions of the structure. Seventeen charcoal samples were found for carbon dating, with 13 rejected for contamination or insufficient quantity. Only one sample seemed to fit the possibility of being present during construction, but a total of four were submitted to a laboratory for analysis. The carbon dates varied from 30 A.D. to 430 A.D. The researchers placed the period of construction of the fort within the Hopewell Indian period of 400 B.C. to 400 A.D. The glaring weakness to their conclusion was that the date of the Hopewell occupation was not known for certain in Tennessee.[6] Were the carbonaceous materials removed from other sites and later utilized at the fort site? Thus far, we suspect that archaeologists have found a very limited and unreliable amount of materials that can be considered relevant for carbon dating at the site.

Such studies start with a basic premise, good scientific intentions, and limited facts to build a case for the time period and builders of the Old Stone Fort. The footnotes of this report stated that, for the sake of American literature, fellow archaeologists had no historical or archaeological evidence of any European migrants in the southeastern interior of the continent during the first five centuries of the Christian Era, and it later implied none before Columbus. These statements continue to be made in spite of many early artifacts found in many areas of the continent.

The same researcher footnoted his statement of prehistoric Indians building the fort with a speculative comment that De Soto encountered the Yuchi tribe within the walls in the 1500s. The mysterious Yuchi tribe, as well as De Soto, will be covered later in our quest for the origin of the Melungeons. He also mentioned the early mound-building Indians as builders of the fort as early as 2000 years ago.[7]

The footnotes continued with the mention of wandering Norsemen in the 10th and 11th centuries and myths of Prince Madoc and the Welshmen in the 12th century. He confirmed that prehistorians had established Vikings as having been in North America before Columbus, but not Madoc, despite recurring reports of blue-eyed Indians speaking a Celtic tongue.[8]

We do know that a plan of the castle of the "Sons of Owain Gwynedd," reported by Giraldi Cambrensis in 1188, bears many identical traits to that of the Old Stone Fort. In spite of limited artifacts found within the walls of the fort, a Roman coin, a denarius of Antonius Pius (138-161 A.D.) was found just south of the fort. The coin was five feet deep and below a 300-400 year old forest.

Another Roman coin, a denarius of Comodus (180-192 A.D.) was found near Fayetteville, Tennessee. Sidney Noe wrote, " The coins were of the second century. We know that during the Roman occupation of Britain, coins were minted in Wales: it is entirely possible that Madoc's twelfth-century colonists brought some of these already ancient coins with them."

A site for a new pond three miles north of Manchester, Tennessee, yielded a chunk of iron ore weighing 2-4 tons. Samples were sent to the Smithsonian Institute for analysis. E. P. Henderson, curator of the meteorite division, examined the mass and reported it to be man-made and not connected with any fallen meteorite. An on-site investigation revealed the mass to be 93% pure iron and similar to materials extracted from Ireland, Germany, and other European areas dating from 900 to 1000 A.D.

Lore has the Madoc descendants migrating out of the Manchester, Tennessee, area to East Tennessee, eventually following the rivers and multiplying. They were found considerably north of the Old Stone Fort at the Falls of the Ohio. The Falls, with its many nearby springs, has been an ideal habitat for life since its discovery by early man. The shallow waters were an excellent habitat for freshwater mussels and abundant fish in the rapids. The center was an ideal crossing for millions of bison who regularly migrated across southern Indiana to the salt flats of Kentucky.

Oral histories of several Native American tribes tell of a large battle at this site between a different type of race and Native Americans. Both the Delaware and the Iroquois speak of the great battle in this coveted area. The Indians eventually prevailed in battle and drove the so-called aborigines to a small island in the river "where the whole of them were cut to pieces." This story was confirmed by George Rogers Clark who stated that there was a large burial ground on the north side of the river just below the falls. Chief Tobacco told Clark of the battle of Sand Island between his people and the inhabitants of what he called "the Dark and Forbidden Land." Indian Chief Cornstalk had a similar story that he reported to Colonel McKee, commander on the Kanawha, of "white people" being the first settlers throughout Tennessee and Kentucky, with knowledge of arts about which the natives knew nothing. He tells of their stone forts, such as the one at Fourteen Mile Creek (page 55) on the Ohio and of known grave sites of these white people of long ago.

Over the years there have also been reports of ancient coins and armor found in the Devil's Backbone area. Some papers have mentioned George Rogers Clark finding skeletons adorned in armor that he believed to be Welshmen. Other early skeletal remains did not seem to be of Native American descent. Artifacts found in the general area included a bronze helmet and arm shield. Smithsonian experts dated the articles at 310-379 A.D. with country of origin as Persia. These items may seem to predate the subjects of our inquiry, but armor was passed from generation to generation in early times; therefore, these pieces may have eventually been carried to America.[9]

Many stories abound concerning a stone fortification on the geologic feature known as the "Devil's Backbone." In his book, *A Journey to the Falls*, Clay Baird states, "Up river from the Falls, near the mouth of Fourteen Mile Creek, there is a stone fortification located about 200 feet above the Ohio River on the "Devil's Backbone." Part of this structure is natural rock and some of it has been laid up by man without the use of mortar. There is speculation that the White Indians at the Falls may have built this fortification, possibly using it in much the same manner that the settlers in this country used stockades and forts for protection against the Red Indians.

American Indians were never known to have erected this type of work out of stone. Since this is the only fortification of its kind in the United States, it is reasonable to speculate that some European visitors were here a long time ago."

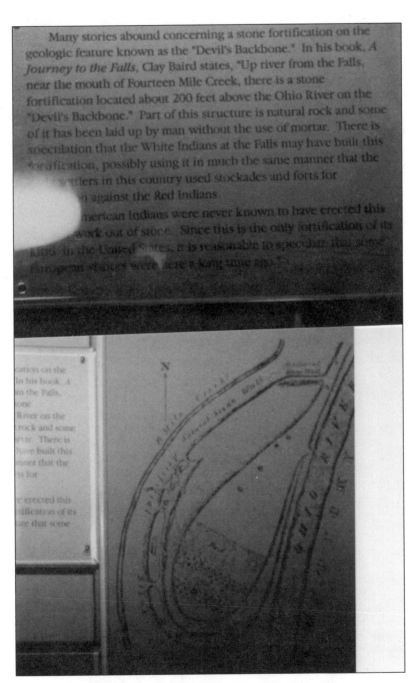

The Fort. Courtesy of Falls of the Ohio Museum

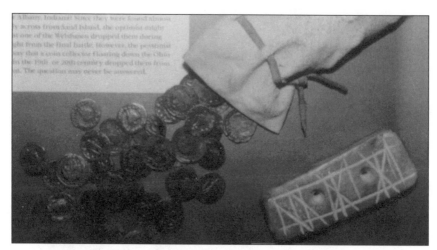

Albany, Indiana. Since they were found almost ... across from [...] Island, the optimist might ... of the Welshmen dropped them during ... from the final battle. However, the pessimist ... that a coin collector floating down the Ohio ... the 19th or 20th century dropped them from ... The question may never be answered.

The Coins. Courtesy of Falls of the Ohio Museum.

The Helmet. Courtesy of Falls of the Ohio Museum

Before leaving this area, we should examine a piece of written documentation. In 1912, the Brandenburg Stone was found near the Ohio River, forty miles from the Falls of the Ohio. As with other stones with ancient inscriptions, this one again defied the ordinary avenues of translation. In 1989, Alan Wilson, a Welsh historian, recognized the markings as Coelbren derived from an early British alphabet. He translated the stone writing as, "Toward strength divide the land we are spread over justly between offspring in wisdom."

The Brandenburg Stone

This stone, with its unusual markings, was discovered in 1912 by Craig Crecelius in his field, below a rocky bluff. The Crecelius farm was near the Ohio River in Paradise Bottoms, just west of Battletown, Kentucky (about 40 miles from the Falls of the Ohio).

The stone remained a mystery, kept in Mr. Crecelius' barn until, with his permission, it was moved to the Brandenburg Library in the 1960's in the hope that someone eventually would be able to identify it. In 1989, members of the Ancient Kentucky Historical Association viewed the stone and noted the similarity to other inscriptions they had seen. They dusted the stone with zinc powder to better show the script, then sent photographs to Alan Wilson, a Welsh historian, who recognized the markings as Coelbren, an ancient British alphabet. His translation reads: "Toward strength (to promote unity) divide the land we are spread over purely (justly) between offspring in wisdom." Later he viewed the stone in person and confirmed this translation.

The Brandenburg Stone. Courtesy of Falls of the Ohio Museum

Deviating from the Welsh in East Tennessee and up to the Ohio, we do find considerable information about the Mandan tribe. They were thought to be descendants of the Welsh, who went north into the Dakotas. Some think the Welsh followed rivers such as the Missouri all the way to this northernmost part of the continent. This tribe was known by Lewis and Clark in their expedition of the early 1800s and contributed immensely to the success of their westward mission under the auspices of Thomas Jefferson.

While Lewis and Clark studied the Mandan, Jefferson was very intrigued by huge earthen mounds being found in eastern North America. He also collected artifacts from such areas for preservation and study. Though he discriminated against most Native Americans, he felt that some superior civilization capable of building the earthen temples, such as the Welsh or others, had existed on the continent prior to their time. Decline or disease may have decimated the more technologically progressive of the people on the continent by the time their activities were recorded for posterity. We do know that most of the large earthen mounds of the East were eventually leveled for cultivation, and Jefferson's extensive Native American collections were sold after his death.

Jefferson, who was of Celtic descent, was very eager to learn about the Mandan Indians during the Lewis and Clark expedition in the early 1800s. He challenged the party to find some Welsh-speaking Indians on the Missouri. More than likely, his Celtic reddish hair and ruddy cheeks along with ethnic pride, subconsciously prompted him to order the investigation of the mysterious Mandans with hopes of establishing the remnants of a former empire discovered by his own people prior to the Spanish.[10]

So what did Lewis and Clark and others observe about the Mandans? In 1721, a Catholic priest named Father Charlevoix heard Iowa Indians speak of fair-haired and white-skinned neighbors three days journey up the river. In 1735, a French explorer named Sier de la Verendrye, visited the Mandan. He noticed their skin was different from other natives and their village was laid out in streets and squares. He left men behind with the Mandan, and they found the Mandan language had many similarities to the Welsh language. Later visitors confirmed Verendrye's observations. One Welshman reported being captured by whites in Indian dress who spared his life when he spoke Welsh. There were many other incidents of Indians that seemed to resemble the Mandan. Some were described as yellow-skinned, light-skinned, sometimes blue-eyed, sometimes lighter reddish-skinned.[11]

George Catlin painted some pictures of the Mandans before they had been exterminated by smallpox, and were no longer identifiable as a people as early as 1840. Catlin had been told when he left

Mandan Beauty. Courtesy of Dover Publications

St. Louis in 1833 that the Mandan were a strange people appearing to be half white. Catlin agreed with his earlier informants. He found them distinctly different from any other tribe he had studied. He noted their hair was finer, more dark brown than black, and that a few had fair hair. He described their eyes as black, brown, and sometimes gray or blue. He described their skin as having many different shades, from yellowish to brown or copperish.

Maximilian, who appeared among the Mandan right after Catlin, ridiculed the tribe's white origin, but he was fascinated with their differences from other tribes. He also described white or yellowish-skinned individuals, others with brown hair, and families with gray hair.

A notable item was the fishing craft of the Mandans. Catlin described them as unlike any used by other tribes. They were made from willows formed like a round tub and covered with skins stretched underneath the frame. This unique craft was the same design as the Welsh wicker coracles (page 46) used even today in Wales.

The craft was propelled by inserting a paddle over the fore-end of the boat with a scooping or figure-eight motion instead of insert-

Coracles. Courtesy of Dana Olson.

ing oars along the sides as was the procedure of other tribes. Catlin even noted a claw carved on the paddle of every boat which is currently present on coracles in the River Trfi in Wales.[12]

The uniqueness of this tribe is well documented. We can even witness Catlin's description of the people celebrating the remembrance of a legendary white man surviving the great flood. In this ritual, they danced around the replica of a nine-foot object representing a great boat. They followed the ceremony with the sacrifice of valuable tools used to build the boat by throwing them into the river to prevent the return of flood waters.[13]

A modern day Mandan story *The Children of First Man* is well written and researched by Indiana author, James Alexander Thom, who published it in 1994. Thom followed the same trails from Mobil to Tennessee to the Dakotas with intriguing suspense. Author Paula Gunn Allen said, "James Alexander Thom has told an old and almost forgotten story about movement between the Americas and the Old World long before Columbus."

Mandan Ceremony. Courtesy of Dover Publications

JAMES ALEXANDER
THOM

Author of
FOLLOW
THE RIVER

The
CHILDREN
of FIRST MAN

The Children of First Man. Courtesy of Ballantine Publishing

Thruston Tablet. Courtesy of Dana Olson

What do we know about the possibility of these people being in East Tennessee or their eventual migration to the more northern areas covered in the preceding paragraphs? Let's take a look at an interesting inscribed stone called the Thruston Tablet found along a tributary of the Cumberland River. The tablet was named after Gates P. Thruston, former secretary of the Tennessee Historical Society, who wrote about the artifact in his book *Antiquities of Tennessee* in 1890.

Some historians had given up on the trail of the white Indians until this stone was found near the mounds of Bledsoe Lick in the area of Castillian Springs. The tablet is nineteen inches in height, fifteen inches in width, and one inch thick. It is on display at the Tennessee State Museum in Nashville.

The writings have been translated as a Viking pictoglyph. Some reject the Viking idea, believing that Vikings could not have been on the inland waters of North America. We look to Madoc and his Viking heritage to erase this minor controversy in an attempt to analyze the significance of this artifact.

There are differences in interpretations of the figures. From the left center, we see an almond-eyed Indian with a type of ax attacking a ray-eyed warrior with a shield and spear. To the right center, we see a well-dressed, almond-eyed female with a wampum marriage belt and a round-eyed warrior with a short, horizontal sword in his left hand. To the right of the couple, we see a ray-eyed man hanging upside down with his heart in his hands, which seems to symbolize the aftermath of battle. The prone figure to the far right and bottom also seems to illustrate a battle with a prone warrior holding out his signal of surrender, a bent spear. At the bottom is a square that appears to be a small hut and a ray-eyed person smoking a pipe, presumably a peace pipe. At the top, we find a Viking-type ship with round-eyed people on board. Three of the depicted subjects are almond-eyed, three are ray-eyed, and the men on the ship are round-eyed. Depicting people of the three eye types was the attempt of the creator to portray races of people intermingling in both battle and unity.

The dress of the subjects seems more primitive than projected in current history books. The square shield and head of the warrior impinged upon the underpinnings of the ship suggests that it was drawn at an earlier time. The stone seems to be aged differently from top to bottom. These observations would lead to the conclusion that the arrival of the ship at the top and subsequent confrontations drawn beneath were not necessarily recorded at the same time.

Upon closer examination, the stone shows an anchor made of metal amidships similar to the anchor of the Oseberg ship, currently housed in the Oslo Museum. Below the tiller post and slightly below the oar holes is a round hole in the side of the hull. Brogger and Shetelig (experts on Viking craft) describe the steering oar of a Viking craft as attached to the hull through a hole in the deck of Viking ships. In line with the tiller post area, there seems to be faint vertical lines and an oval shape that were probably erased as the engraver drew the elaborate headdress of the subject just below the ship.

Who were these people represented on the Thurston Tablet? We know that Bledsoe Lick was a center for early Indians. When whites first came into the area, they found no Indians. Surrounding tribes were using the area as a shared hunting ground but understood a people had lived in the area with an advanced form of civilization prior to their period. Archaeologists have found supporting evidence of such an advanced people from the numerous assortment of mounds, earthworks, flint tools, and pottery fragments found nearby.[14]

We must leave Madoc, Mandans, and Welsh Indians as inconclusive but thought-provoking questions. We have not concluded whether the Welsh were early Melungeons, early Mandans, or Welsh Indians, but we are deeply suspicious of the Welsh role in the settlement of the continent. Columbus was very perceptive when, on his second voyage, he observed three ancient wrecked ships of European design near Guadelope. Peter Martyr of Anghiera, an Italian geographer and historian who was present in King Ferdinand's court when Columbus returned home, writes in his documents called "De Orbe De Cades Octo" of Columbus's comments on a key map. Columbus wrote "Questo he Mar de Cambrio," meaning these are Welsh waters.[15]

[1]Dana Olson, *Prince Madoc: Founder of Clark County, Indiana*, Jeffersonville, Indiana, 1987, pp. 4-6.

[2]Jean Patterson Bible, *Melungeons Yesterday and Today*, East Tennessee Printing Company, Rogerville, Tennessee, 1975, p. 81.

[3]Roger G. Kennedy, *Hidden Cities*, Penguin Books, New York, New York, 1994, p. 234.

[4]Zella Armstrong, *Who Discovered America? The Amazing Story of Madoc*, Chattanooga, Lookout Publishing Company, 1950, p. 8.

[5]Charles H. Faulkner, *The Old Stone Fort*, The University of Tennessee Press, Knoxville, Tennessee, 1968, p. 23.

[6]ibid, p. 23-25.

[7]ibid, p. 8.

[8]ibid, p. 8.

[9]Dana Olson, *Prince Madoc: Founder of Clark County, Indiana*, Jeffersonville, Indiana, 1987, pp. 49- 63.

[10]Roger G. Kennedy, *Hidden Cities*, Penguin Books, New York, New York, 1994, pp. 231-236.

[11]*Mysteries of The Ancient Americas*, Readers DigestAssociation, Inc., Pleasantville, New York, 1990, pp. 34-35.

[12]Dana Olson, pp. 96-97.

[13]*Mysteries of The Ancient Americas*, p. 35.

[14]Dana Olson, pp. 54-56.

[15]ibid, p. 25.

Chapter 6
Moors & Berbers

Some have expounded upon the theory of the Melungeons being from North Africa. We lack proof of this theory, but the premise is valid enough for further examination. The source of the people, for this part of our investigation, will be in the vicinity of present-day Morocco and other parts of the north shore of Africa. Note the map of Morocco and its close proximity to Spain, Portugal, and the

Present-Day Morocco. Courtesy of Alfred A. Knopf, Inc.

earlier empire of the Phoenicians. We have discussed the Phoenicians, and we will now see how this group of later North African people also figured into the puzzle of the possible source of the Melungeons.

The earliest group to be considered are the Berbers. The Phoenicians encountered the ancestors of current Berber-speaking people when they first explored the region. Berbers are presently described as the native Caucasian, non-Arabic population of North Africa with their own language. Caves near Casablanca revealed stone tools of these people dated as early as 800,000 B.C., but outsiders from the Near East eventually joined the early tribes to become hybrid ancestors of the present Berbers.[1] It seems the Saraha Desert to the south was more of a barrier in early times than the Mediterranean Sea to the north because of the eventual intermingling and appearances of the African people.

Berbers are described physically as short, dark-haired, dark-eyed, light-skinned, and round-headed, and are classified racially as Mediterranean Caucasoids with a Negro admixture. Blond hair, blue eyes, long heads, and tall statures are occasionally found north of the Saraha Desert, but these traits are not the norm. Culturally, linguistically, and racially the North Africans are tied to Europe

Berber Youth. Courtesy of P.R. Collier & Sons.

and the Middle East.[2]

The written historical period of these people began in 800-600 B.C. according to script invented by the Berbers, found in the Atlas Mountains. In this same time period, pottery found offshore on the island of Essaouire (see map page 66) was identified as having Phoenician lettering. About 100 years later, Ethiopians from farther east settled in the area, as sedentary people in the North and hunting nomads in the South. In between these groups lived the people called the Atlantes, after whom the Atlantic Ocean is named.

With Berber being their basic origin, the people were later called Mauri, Maurusian, or Moors by the Greeks. They were eventually ruled as a colony by the Romans from sometime after Rome conquered Carthage in 146 B.C. until the late 600s A.D. Rome was aware of their influence in Spain and Morocco and understood the importance of their influence in controlling all trade through the Straits of Gibraltar. The Roman plan allowed a Berber king, Juba ll, to rule from 25 B.C. until 23 A.D. Juba II ruled through his marriage of convenience to the Roman daughter of Marc Anthony and Cleopatra. The Berbers prospered under his reign. Caligula, the next Roman emperor, did not trust the loose governmental situation and conquered Morocco in 42 A.D. He mandated that the country be direct subjects of Rome. He then divided the kingdom into two provinces to dilute the power of the Berbers, and it remained divided until 285 A.D. in the South and 429 A.D. in the North.

The Romans were challenged by the Goths and Vandals from Germany. The people overran Roman Spain and parts of North Africa by 429 A.D. The Byzantine Empire then tried to follow the Romans and conquer the people of Morocco and failed — leaving the natives to battle among themselves for control of Morocco.

At this time, the Berbers consisted of three major tribes. The Masmoudas lived on the coast and in the Atlas Mountains and were generally farmers. The Sanhajas were warlike nomads who lived south, extending to the black kingdom of Senegal. They were proficient and dependent upon camels for mobility. The third tribe, the Zenatas, lived in eastern Morocco and preferred horses for transportation. They were excellent cavalrymen. These three fierce and warlike tribes battled for the next two hundred years for domination of Morocco.[3]

In 682 A.D., the situation changed once again, as Arab raiders known as Muslims began to invade Morocco from the East. Their inspiration was the spiritual leader and prophet Muhammad in Mecca. All new Muslim conquests were fought for their God, Allah. Muhammad died in 632 A.D., but his influence lived far into the future, as zealous followers battled for the glory of Muhammad and Allah. All battles were initiated with, "There is no God but Allah and Muhammad is his Prophet." By 701 A.D., vast hordes of men on horses and camels had conquered most of Morocco. The term Moor became a description of the mixture of Berbers and the conquering Arabs; therefore, the country of Morocco had Berbers with various degrees of intermingling with Arabs who now were identified as Arabs, Moors, or Berbers.

After the conquest, many Berbers decided to join the Muslims, and the new union looked for countries to forcibly convert. The next step for the love of Allah was to cross the straits of Gibraltar to attack Christian Spain. This new and zealous united front was immediately able to establish a foothold in southern Spain in the province of Andalusia. Surprisingly, a period of mutual harmony and acceptance followed the domination of Spain. Eventually, religion again dominated race as the Berbers declined in importance and were treated unfairly by ruling Muslims. The Berbers became embittered with what they had expected to be a long and equal partnership; thus, they split away from Muslim rule, never to be controlled again by the Arabs of the East.

The unified Berbers under Tariq, a true Berber leader, crossed the straits to Spain again in 711 A.D. and rallied the troops toward Toledo and on to the Pyrenees Mountains. Tariq and the Berbers crossed the mountains and occupied southern France, but the area around Asturias and Cantabria remained Christian.

The union of Islamic Berbers and Spanish Christians was a continual problem. The Spanish were encouraged to convert to Islam and could only retain their faith for a fee. Others did convert and even changed their names. These volunteer converts were considered traitors to the Spanish religion and were labeled "renegados" by their own people.

For the next four hundred years, there were many conflicts within Spain as the strengths of the conquering Islamic Berbers

Berber Spain. Courtesy P. R. Collier & Son Corporation

waned, and the conquered Spanish Christians either weakened or prospered. The long period of fighting between the two faiths eventually had a profound effect upon the Spanish people. The constant segmentation caused by their adversaries intensified a lack of disunity, but it fostered a strong fanatical sense of religion and patriotism. Their long fragmentation also caused extreme desires for wealth and power. These cultural attributes carried through into their ideas of colonization in the Americas.

The Spanish prevailed as the Inquisition began in 1237. The Roman Catholic Church began a concentrated effort to discover, examine, and purge all known heretics from the country. This had a profound effect on Moors in Spain.

The Spanish survived the long tumultuous period, and by 1474, change was again forthcoming. The king, Henry IV of Spain, had died and was succeeded by his daughter, Isabella. She married Prince Ferdinand of Aragon and eventually regained control of her country. Many reforms were imposed for the betterment of the Spanish people, but the Inquisition became state controlled by 1480 and remained so until 1834. Ferdinand and Isabella supported the persecution of many, but her insights into exploration were a positive force. Her support of the Christopher Columbus voyages resulted in Spain becoming a new colonial empire.[4]

King Ferdinand and Queen Isabella drove many of the Moors/Berbers, Moriscos (Spanish Muslims), and Jews from Spain during their reign to cleanse Catholic Spain of all undesirable non-Christians. The entire period of persecution and upheaval might have caused fleeing or removal, and subsequent relocation, of outcasts to the North American continent.

Slavery was common in the Mediterranean world in the thirteenth and fourteenth centuries. It is possible that the Berber/Moorish people became early settlers via slavery on the North American continent. In Iberia, Islamic laws recognized slavery, and Muslims could even hold their own in slavery if they were black or loro, an intermediate color between black and white.[5]

In neighboring Portugal, records show Muslim slaves as early as the thirteenth century, along with Mocarabes (Christians living in a fashion similar to surrounding Arabs). During this time, Portuguese were raiding the Canary Islands to obtain Canarios, as well as Muslims, for trade. In the fifteenth century, Berbers and black Senegalese slaves were common, especially after 1440-50.[6]

We do know that Christopher Columbus failed in his quest for precious metals but found slavery to be lucrative. He sent 3,000 to 6,000 slaves from America to Europe, from the Azores, Canaries,Madeira, and Cambo Verde Islands. We do not know if he exported others in the opposite direction, but by 1500, the Spanish and Portuguese had escalated the trade in slavery throughout their areas of influence.[7] In the fourteenth and fifteenth centuries, records were found of slavery in the Iberian Peninsula, North Africa, and vicinity. Numerous preserved records list Berber/Moorish slaves being bought and sold. The earlier lists identified them as colored or loros, and by the 1550s, they were described as mulatto.[8]

The theory of the Melungeons being descendants of Moors is also a consideration based on a voyage of Sir Francis Drake in 1585. On this particular voyage, Drake departed England on September 14th with twenty-five ships and 2,300 soldiers and mariners. He proceeded south along the Iberian coast pilfering Spanish ships before attempting to take on water and supplies in the Canary Islands. He was surprised by heavy Spanish artillery near the

Moorish Woman. Courtesy of the Grolier Society, Inc.

Island of Palma and fled on toward the Cape Verde archipelago and the island of Sao Tiago. Here he disembarked a thousand soldiers as a dress rehearsal for looting riches in New Spain across the Atlantic. His new crewmen responded well and learned from the small invasion experience; however, the men were at sea only a few days before sickness and death struck. The expedition's chronicler, Captain Walter Biggs, reported that "wee were not many dayes at Sea, but there beganne among our people such mortalitie, as in a few days there were dead above two or three hundred men. In some that died were plainley shewed the small spots, which are often found upon those that be infected with the plague."[9]

In spite of disease, Drake and his men crossed the Atlantic, seized Santo Domingo and Cartagena, but dropped plans to attack the viceroyalty of New Spain in Panama. He failed to wrest ransoms from the Spanish governors of either Santo Domingo or Cartagena, aborted a plan to loot the Spanish mines in Honduras, and then headed north to attack St. Augustine. By this time, St. Augustine had been established for twenty-two years as a result of the abandonment by the French of their Fort Caroline thirty miles to the north. This was the last French attempt to settle in Florida.

Drake's forces attacked and burned Fort San Juan and vulnerable St. Augustine. They landed long enough to salvage any windows or hardware that might have been useful in the colony of Roanoke. The fleet also captured armament and any other looted objects of value for England. Upon arrival in the colony, Drake also expected to warn the colonists of the growing Spanish threat from the south. His pirating activities certainly did not enhance public relations with the Spanish![10]

Drake's activities took a toll upon his leadership of the tired and diseased soldiers. The crew consisted of freed and captured people that were trying to live and survive. One report listed 1,200 Englishmen, Frenchmen, and Flemings, as well as eight hundred "of the countrey people."[11] Other sources said this country list included Moorish and Turkish slaves, runaway Indians, and blacks of unknown origin.

Some say Drake planned to leave the miscellaneous cargo of miserable humans with the smaller boats at a fort near Roanoke called Jacan. Jacan was directly west of Bermuda and 250 leagues from the Spanish colony of Santa Elena. It was built to enable its occupants to attack selected enemy fleets in any season.[12]

Drake knew an initial fleet sent to resupply the colonists was diverted to Newfoundland, but he thought a second fleet had been sent to Virginia with sufficient supplies for his unloading of surplus slaves at Jacan. Upon contact with authorities at Roanoke, Drake found that they had not been resupplied and had no desire for any additional refugees. The two parties compromised, with Drake offering to leave a small ship for local exploration, a few provisions, and a few skilled craftsmen. By this time, the hurricane season was imminent, and a strong storm occurred on June 13. The small ship left for the colonists was sunk, and by June 16, the storm was still raging. In spite of Drake offering a larger ship to the colonists, they were all ready to return to England. Records are vague, but many believe the colonists departed with Drake and the slaves were sent ashore to survive on their own intuitions. This would possibly place Moors and others in the colony in 1586. These people could have been the original nucleus of later Melungeons.

Let us analyze a more recent attempt to genetically connect the Melungeons to a North African ancestry. Over the years, numerous scientific analyses have been conducted on blood and genes of Melungeons. We will not discuss earlier studies, as availability of materials and methods have improved over time. Studies, as mentioned earlier by Pollitzer and Brown, concluded that they were of a Caucasoid population with little evidence of Negroid or Amerindian influence. The study did not refute the popular, longtime theories of a triracial isolate or even the Melungeons calling themselves "Portugee."

In 1990, James Guthrie

Sir Francis Drake
Courtesy of Ivor Noel Hume

approached the Melungeon gene study with newer technology and resources. His intention was to study Melungeon origins with no consideration of current theories of origin and with only published gene frequency distributions as the data base. He used worldwide tabulations by A. E. Mourant (1976) and his associates (Tills, Kopec, and Tills, 1983). All of his scientific details are available for those deeply interested in procedures and methods. Guthrie compared data of five blood groups as a simplified but uniform method for estimating genetic differences or similarities between pairs of populations.

Guthrie listed the MMD (mean method of divergence) of 36 of the closest populations of a total of 100. These were considered in diminishing similarity from the Melungeons. Racial and regional designations are those of A.E. Mourant. The column (N2) designates ranges to reflect data collected by different workers within the same geographical area. The corrected MMD column reflects an adjustment for different sample sizes and is our final guide for analysis of the study.

There are 12 populations in the corrected MMD column with values of 0.030 or less. Six of those 12 do not differ from the Melungeon sample at the 95% confidence level (p = 0.05). These countries are marked by asterisk. Guthrie qualified the study by concluding that the similar samples were from a distinct northwestern coast of Europe or the Mediterranean, except for the Minnesota sample. He also qualifies the sample by Mourant from Italy as not representative of too many populations in only two or three blood systems.

Guthrie qualified the study in that small sample sizes were used with uneven distributions. They were also qualified with changes in gene frequency over time, and the limited availability of Melungeon data for only five systems. He summarized the study by concluding that populations not significantly different from the Melungeons still exist, and they are found in a well-defined part of the world.[13]

In spite of irrefutable proof, it appears that people from North Africa could have been involved in self-imposed migrations in the 1400s-1600s or involved as slaves during the same period. People of these areas, as confirmed genetically by Guthrie, were on a prime slave-trading route for ships crossing the Atlantic to the New World.[13]

Mean Measure of Divergence of Melungeons from Other Populations			
		MMD and SD	
Population	N,(range)	Uncorrected	Corrected
Libya (Tripoli)	138-2862	0.028±0.020	0.017±0.022*
Canary Islands	182-277	0.029±0.031	0.019±0.031*
Malta	117-164	0.030±0.025	0.018±0.025*
Portugal	302-4767	0.031±0.022	0.024±0.022
Italy (Veneto)	126-606	0.034±0.033	0.022±0.035*
Ireland	>2000	0.035±0.052	0.029±0.052
Italy (Trentino)	149-383	0.036±0.011	0.026±0.012*
Italy	>6000	0.036±0.026	0.030±0.026
Sweden	>5000	0.036±0.033	0.030±0.033
U.S. Whites (Minnesota)	240-300	0.037±0.040	0.28±0.040
Libya (minus Fezzan)	218-3100	0.037±0.033	0.030±0.033
Britain	>4000	0.037±0.028	0.031±0.028
Cyprus (Troodos)	67	0.038±0.035	0.017±0.034*
Germany (Sacchsen)	>2500	0.038±0.026	0.031±0.026
Greece	148-3587	0.038±0.021	0.032±0.021
Netherlands	>1500	0.038±0.026	0.032±0.026
Spain (Galicia)	76-231	0.040±0.029	0.027±0.027*
Wales	116-1289	0.041±0.047	0.033±0.043
Corsica	132-1937	0.042±0.033	0.034±0.032
France	132-17,000	0.042±0.028	0.035±0.026
Spain	580-5200	0.042±0.037	0.036±0.037
U.S. Whites	>10,000	0.042±0.034	0.036±0.034
England	>3000	0.046±0.041	0.040±0.041
Iceland	135-2400	0.049±0.047	0.041±0.048
Sicily	107-2694	0.050±0.043	0.040±0.043
Northern Ireland	315-723	0.051±0.040	0.042±0.040
Finland (Häme)	627-970	0.053±0.072	0.046±0.084
Sardinia	644-2475	0.059±0.050	0.051±0.050
Cyprus	193-448	0.068±0.037	0.058±0.037
Turkey	108	0.068±0.062	0.053±0.062
Catawba (mixed)	104	0.121±0.091	0.108±0.088
U.S. Blacks	>2500	0.195±0.098	0.189±0.098
Gullah (Blacks, SC, used by Pollitzer)	125-665	0.230±0.237	0.222±0.238
Seminole, Oklahoma	224	0.250±0.247	0.241±0.246
Cherokee	78	0.274±0.234	0.256±0.234
Seminole, Florida	381	0.316±0.252	0.308±0.252

* means not significantly different at the 95% confidence level. SD is standard deviation of the five blood group values (see appendix).

Guthrie Comparisons. Courtesy of Tennessee Anthropologist.

[1]*Morocco*, Alfred A. Knopf, Inc. New York, New York, 1994, p. 52.

[2]*Collier Encyclopedia*, P. F. Collier and Son, Corp., New York, New York, 1952, Volume 1, p. 168.

[3]Martin Hintz, *Morocco*, Regensteiner Publishing Enterprises, Inc., Chicago, 1985.

[4]*Morocco*, Alfred A. Knopf, Inc.

[5]Yce de Chebir, *Memorial Historico Espanol*, Madrid, 1853, Volume 5, pp. 334-368.

[6]A. H. de Oliveira Marques, *History of Portugal*, Columbia University Press, New York, 1972, pp. 55-80.

[7]Jack D. Forbes, *Africans and Native Americans*, University of Illinois Press,

Chicago, Illinois, 1993, p. 28.

[8]ibid p. 1559.

[9]Hakluyt, "A summarie and true discourse of sir Francis Drakes West India voyage, begun in the yeere 1585." volume Vll, p. 87.

[10]Ivor Noel Hume, *The Virginia Adventure*, University Press of Virginia, Charlottesville, Virginia, 1994

[11]"Turks, Moors, Blacks, and Others in Drake's West India Voyage," Terrae Incognitae, Volume 14, 1982, p. 94, Letter of Nickolas Cleaver to Nicholas Turner, May 26, 1586

[12]Wright, *Further English Voyages to Spanish America 1583-1594*, p. 204: Diego Fernandez de Quinones to the Crown, Havana, September 1586

[13]James L. Guthrie, "Melungeons: Comparisons of Gene Frequency," Tennessee Anthropologist, Volume XV, Number 1, Spring 1990

Chapter 7
The Spanish and Portuguese,
Also the Yuchi and a Few French

We need to briefly study the history between the two major people in this chapter, the Spanish and Portuguese, in order to understand why they will be considered as possible Melungeon sources. Racially, the Portuguese and Spanish are descended from the same round-headed Iberian people. Both were dominated by Moors from the eighth to the thirteenth centuries.

Portuguese control of the African coast during the early modern period contributed to the more extensive mixing with Negroid people and a definite increase in the Negroid strain within all the Celtberian (Celt Iberian) people of Portugal. This deviation did not make an overall visible difference between the people of the two countries.

Portugal was actually an artificial creation of the Iberian Peninsula. Early visitors indiscriminately touched the coasts of both Spain and Portugal. The Greeks had colonies at the mouths of both the To and Dour Rivers.

The Romans followed with control of the Iberian southeast and later moved north and west to control modern Portugal. Portugal was eventually absorbed into the Roman provinces of Lusitania and Glacier. Under the Romans, the Portuguese were thoroughly Latinized and achieved full citizenship by 210 A.D. In this period, all their aboriginal languages were replaced by Latin and gradually disappeared with little trace.

By 500 A.D., additional changes began to be significant, as both Spain and Portugal were invaded by Germanic tribes from the North; however, this period of oppression was short-lived, as the new Visigothic Period was about to begin. Goths, the invaders in this new era of repression, were originally from southern Sweden but of Germanic origin. These people conquered Rome, and even Athens, before being driven out by determined armies and leadership.

By 376 A.D., the Goths were back in Roman territory and, once again, defeated the Romans at Adrianople. After the death of their leader, Theodosius, they moved first to Rome in 410 and then turned westward, toward the Iberian Peninsula. The entire peninsula was eventually conquered by a tribe of the West Goths, or The Visigoths. The East Goths, or Ostrogoths, did not cross the Danube during the invasion of the Peninsula and were eventually defeated by the Huns.

The Visigoths ruled the Iberian peninsula for three hundred years, and they contributed to a general cultural decline before

CULVER SERVIC

BATTLE OF THE SPANIARDS WITH THE MOORS
FROM A WOOD ENGRAVING

Spanish Battle Moors. Courtesy of Brittanica.

being conquered by the Moors in 711 A.D.[1] As covered in the last chapter, the Muslim era was now beginning and the prophet, Muhammad of Mecca, inspired the Muslim Arabs to overrun Persia, Syria, Palestine, and Egypt. Arabs then headed west to conquer the fierce and warlike Berbers in 695 A.D. The Berbers split away to follow Tariff onward to Toledo and to conquer the bulk of the Iberian Peninsula. What is the significance of returning to this event of occupation by the Moors by now mixed with the Arabs of Eastern Africa? This was the probable period of skin darkening by the people of the Iberian Peninsula.

Racial mixing and religious absorption continued for six hundred years, but the Iberian Peninsula people rose once more to challenge their conquerors. The Spanish Inquisition period of the 1300s in Argon and throughout Spain by 1478 strengthened and inspired the native Christians to drive out the Muslim Moors. The last were out of Spain by 1609-1611.

Portugal became independent in 1143 just prior to the Inquisition, and by 1279, they were the size and configuration of today. They were helped in their own battles to expel the Moors by the English, Fleming, and others from Europe. Again in 1580, they were absorbed by Spain until they revolted and were freed in 1640.[2]

The Iberian Peninsula, after this period, was mixed with Phoenician, Carthaginian, Iberian, Roman, Moor, Jew, English, Dutch, Barbarian tribes, and, eventually, many Negro slaves from Africa. Physical comparisons are frequently subjective, but the following picture of Alfonso X111, King of Spain 1886-1931 is the result of the above mixtures; alongside are similar appearing Melungeons, John Mullins Jr. 1855-1925 and below Munlas Collins 1875-1932.

The Spanish overseas empire began with the voyages of Christopher Columbus, who was thought to have discovered a new route to India by sailing west. This event led to the Treaty of Tordesillas in 1494, which delineated the world's spheres on a line of demarcation, with the Portuguese legally to the east of the new treaty line. The line inadvertently gave the advantage of Brazil to the Portuguese. This imaginary boundary was 370 leagues west of the Cape Verde Islands. This treaty, and the supposition of the Columbus discovery of a new passageway to India, motivated the Portuguese to search for a different route to the Far East. Vasco Da

Spanish King & Melungeons. Courtesy of National Geographic Society
John Mullins, Jr. Courtesy of John Mullins III (deceased) Aileen Mullins
Munlas Collins, Courtesy of Isa Mae McCay (deceased) C.M. (Jerry) Collins

Gama sailed around Africa to India in 1497-98.

This launched a long period of sea exploration, power, and successes by both Spain and Portugal. Portugal initially lagged behind Spain, as they preferred the lucrative trade of the "Spice Islands" of the Orient and Africa to inland exploration of North America. Within a few years of the first discoveries, either country had several opportunities to transplant isolated citizens to North America. In most instances, it would have been impossible to definitively identify the visual difference between a person of either Spanish or Portuguese origin, for they lived under the same circumstances in the same general area for a long period.

In 1521, just 29 years after the discovery of America by Columbus, Francisco Girdle, with ships supplied by Lucas Vasquez de Allyson, departed Santo Domingo (Dominican Republic) in search of slaves. He combined forces in Abaci with Padre de Quexo, who was capitalized by Orates de Matinees. They joined forces and headed north to look for a giant people reported five years earlier. They entered the Jordan River (since identified as the Santa) and found the Indian village, where they traded for three days, took possession of the property in the names of their patrons, and loaded 60 unwilling inhabitants.

Girdle's ship foundered, the slaves were transferred to Quexo's, and Girdle limped home to Spain. The large-statured Indians did not fare well as slave material as most died very quickly in Santo Domingo.

Meanwhile, back in Spain, the men subsidizing the two caravels, Allyson and Matinees, each sued for their own recognized possession of the new lands. By 1525,. Allyson sent Quexo out again toward America with two caravels to survey the unknown lands. Allyson envisioned finding treasure equal to the earlier riches found in Mexico and Peru. Quexo sailed for months and covered 500 miles of the coast, all the way to the Bay of the Mother of God (Chesapeake). A map of his voyage painted by Juan Vespucci, nephew of Amerigo, survives today.

The courts were still scrutinizing the lawsuit between Allyson and Matinees, in July 1526, when Allyson dispatched six ships with 500 men, women, children, soldiers, priests, and the first black slaves to America. The terrain was to be navigated by one of the previously giant slaves taken by Girdle named Francisco de Choicer, after his land of origin. The flagship went aground on the shoals of the Santa river with the supplies for the expedition. The survivors were taken ashore by Francis de Choicer, who immediately disappeared upon returning home.

Allyson moved the disoriented passengers down the coast 150 miles to build the first European settlement in the present United States; he called it San Mogul de Gualdape.

By fall, 200 persons had been interred into graves. By October 18,

Quexo Map. Courtesy Colliers' Encyclopedia.

1526, Allyson died, and mutiny ensued in the settlement. Only 150 persons returned to Spain. The only records we have of the ill-fated attempt is the map above with the words "land of Allyson." Archaeologists are still searching for the settlement. The survivors of such an expedition would be the foremost subjects of our study.

La Florida became the name of the New World Spanish empire, stretching from Key West to the St. Lawrence and from the Atlantic to the Pacific. As a result of the failure of the colony of Allyson, King Philip II of Spain allowed a generation of time to pass before considering settlements again in North America. In the meantime, Nerves, Horned de Soot, Triton de Ulna, and Villafane searched the perimeters of the continent for wealth and new opportunities.[3]

Probably the most familiar explorer of the two countries would be Hernando De Soto in 1538-43. He followed the prevailing trade winds and landed in Tampa Bay with over 600 men. De Soto rapidly headed northward to search for the fulfillment of the longtime Spanish obsession with gold and silver. In this intriguing story covering more than 3,500 miles, we tend to forget the vastness of the entire New World and the unlimited control of Spain over La Florida, their empire.[4]

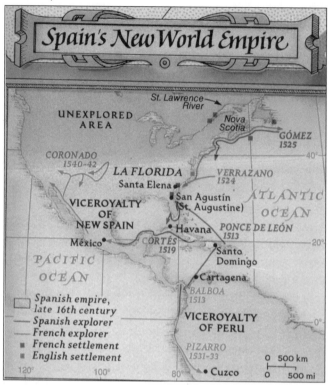

Spain's New World Empire

St. Lawrence River

UNEXPLORED AREA

Nova Scotia

GÓMEZ 1525

40°

CORONADO 1540-42

LA FLORIDA
Santa Elena

VERRAZANO 1524

ATLANTIC OCEAN

VICEROYALTY OF NEW SPAIN

San Agustín (St. Augustine)

México

CORTÉS 1519

Havana

PONCE DE LEÓN 1513

20°

PACIFIC OCEAN

Santo Domingo

Cartagena

BALBOA 1513

Spanish empire, late 16th century
Spanish explorer
French explorer
French settlement
English settlement

VICEROYALTY OF PERU

PIZARRO 1531-33

0°

120°   100°   80°   Cuzco

0   500 km
0   500 mi

Spain's New World Empire. Courtesy of National Geographic.

Although it is difficult to establish the exact route of De Soto, archaeological digs produced Spanish artifacts identified with his period and named aboriginal tribes in conjunction with their respective locations, thus giving us a fairly good route of De Soto and his soldiers.[5]

Hernando de Soto

Driven by a vain search for gold, he and his Spanish expedition became in 1541 the first Europeans to see the Mississippi River as they explored westward from Florida.
CORBIS-BETTMANN, NEW YORK CITY

Hernando De Soto
Courtesy of National Geographic

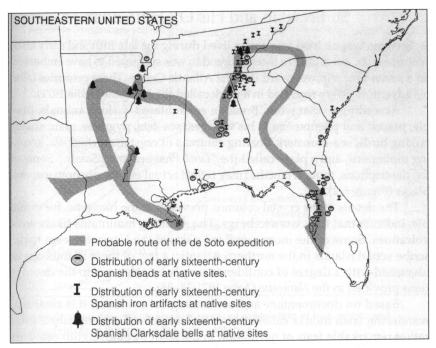

SOUTHEASTERN UNITED STATES

▬ Probable route of the de Soto expedition

◉ Distribution of early sixteenth-century
Spanish beads at native sites.

I Distribution of early sixteenth-century
Spanish iron artifacts at native sites

🔔 Distribution of early sixteenth-century
Spanish Clarksdale bells at native sites

Probable Route of De Soto. Courtesy of Kenneth L. Freder.

Archaeological evidence symbolized on the map illustrates a trail of Neuter Cadiz beads, brass bells, silver and gold discs, along with assorted iron objects such as scissors, swords, and even dated coins. Neuter Cadiz beads were found in northwestern Georgia, the Martin site in Florida, and in a village identified as the Anhaica Indians of Appalachia. Wrought-iron nails, chain mail links, a crossbow dart, and five Spanish coins that date to an earlier Spanish expedition were also found at the Martin site.[6]

We will trace DeSoto onward, but we need to acknowledge his encounters with the Yuchi Indians prior to reaching the northernmost point. More than once, we note the mention of the Yuchi tribes in the context of De Soto's explorations northward toward Tennessee. As mentioned in the Prince Madoc theory of the Melungeons, De Soto is said to have encountered and battled the Yuchi tribe entrenched in the Old Stone Fort at Manchester, Tennessee. These people were called Ani-Yutsi, Chicks, Haughty, Rickohockan, Tamahita, Tsoyaha (people of the sun) or West by various other people in the Southeast.[7] One of the more intriguing names is the Tsoyaha Yuchi, meaning, "We are the children of the sun from far away." Those not accepting this claim of divine ancestry merely called them Yuchi, or "faraway people."

The Yuchi were noted for the uniqueness of their language among the Southeastern Indians as well as their warlike tendencies. De Soto battled them, as did the Spaniard Juan Pardo several years later. De Soto's connection with the Yuchi continued northward in his search of exploitation in the form of gold and silver. De Soto heard of another Yuchi tribe in the province of Chic, and he sent scouts for verification. The scouts returned with reports of a narrow trail over the mountains too treacherous for the expedition to attempt. The Spanish scouts reported the Yuchi utilized brass kettles and arms that they assumed to be stolen from the Spanish arsenal far to the south in St. Augustine, Florida. Others familiar with the Yuchi attributed the advanced metalworking skills directly to the tribe. Some reported their having mines for the smelting of metal. Such stories are repeated over and over in the lore of the early Melungeon history, as smelting and coin production are also a part of their mysterious history.

Benjamin Hawking, United States Commissioner to the Creeks, reported the Yuchi in 1785 as being "more civilized and orderly than their neighbors. The women are more chaste, and the men better hunters." He continues, "They have lately begun to settle out in the villages, and are industrious, compared with their neighbors. The men help the women in their labors, and are more constant in their attachment to the women than usual among the red people."

In 1791, William Bertram, a botanist, visited a Yuchi settlement on the Chattahoochee River, in search of botanical specimens. He described the largest, most compact, and best organized town he had seen among Native American villages. He said, "The houses had wooden frames, latched and plastered inside and out with a reddish, well-tempered clay, or mortar, that looked like red brick walls. They were nearly covered with cypress bark and shingles."[8]

A later descendant of a British and Yuchi marriage reported Yuchi features of gray eyes, lighter complexions than other aboriginal people, different facial features, and many beautiful women.[9]

Some believed them to be originally from Andorra Island in the

Bahamas. When confronted by Christopher Columbus and guns, they were believed to have fled to the mainland. Another theory was by Chief Samuel Brown, Jr.(1879-1957) of the Yuchi. From descriptions by his grandfather, he deduced that the Yuchi had inhabited Georgia for 1000 years, and that they had lived in a coastal area prior to Georgia that had since submerged. He also knew of the possibility that the Yuchi were the original inhabitants of Easter Island, west of Chile.[10]

Understanding this deviation from the continual route of De Soto toward Tennessee is necessary in order to introduce the Yuchi and to attempt some sort of Spanish linkage with this unique tribe of Indians. Such is the case with the Maenads who also differed from all the other surrounding tribes. Eventually, they were all killed in battles with the Spanish or absorbed by Creeks and Seminoles, until the remnants moved to Oklahoma with the Creeks. Very little has been recorded for history that would enable us to further examine any connection to these people.

We know that De Soto survived the Yuchis and continued his search, maybe as far northward as East Tennessee, before turning south and west to attempt to return to Spanish Mexico. By this time, wars, pestilence, and weariness had decimated his onetime formidable army of 600 men and his supplies. Perhaps some men were captured or had mutinied along the treacherous route. Some may have intentionally been left behind in order to preserve limited supplies. Some may have been attracted to the beauty of Native Americans after such a long period in the wilderness. The lighter skinned Yuchis might have been attractive to the male individuals of such a sexually deprived group. A hybrid of such a union might even be called "tawny" colored, as was descriptive of the Melungeons.

More recently (1975), Jean Paterson Bible interviewed Martha Collins, now deceased, a prominent Melungeon from Hancock County, Tennessee, about her opinion of her family's origin (page 89). Martha reiterated the De Soto story, as carried in her family by Uncle J. G. Rhea. A letter written on February 18, 1918, by Mr. Rhea, in old-fashioned script on faded yellow paper, theorized their early descendants may have been Portuguese-Spanish. He thought they were descendants of the followers of De Soto's fruitless search from Florida to Tennessee for gold and silver. He writes of some of them being captured, lost, or befriended by the Indians of the region, intermarring with Indian women, and leaving genes that contributed to the many darker-colored persons of the counties of Rhea, Hancock, Hawkins, and the adjoining counties of Western Virginia.[11]

Local historians and citizens always gave considerable credence to the branches of the Martha Collins clan, which included the Rhea branch of her Uncle J.G. Rhea. Martha, born 1895, daughter of Commodore "Bud" Collins and granddaughter of Bailey Collins (son of Solomon) and Melissa Rhea, served as president of the Sneedville Bank in Hancock County, Tennessee, until her 80th birthday. This branch of the Collins family was one of the first to leave the isolated and unproductive areas of Newsman's Ridge to live among white settlers along the fertile Clinch River. They were rumored to have paid for their fertile farms with gold, which is a part of the lore of the Melungeons.

Another letter of Uncle J. G. Rhea spoke of a more recent Melungeon in the history of the Hancock County area known as Navaho Collins. Later, he was referred to as Yardmen (Vary) Collins. Ms. Bible pondered the significance of the frequent Portuguese spelling

Melissa Rhea Collins with Frank Mullins.
Courtesy of Helen Mullins (deceased) Billie Mullins Horton.

Martha Collins- about 1913.
Courtesy of Martha Collins (deceased) Georgia Collins Weatherred

of "navarrah" for the word "yardmen." She wondered if perhaps earlier educated Melungeons adopted the word to support the idea of a Portuguese origin.[12] Many early pioneers may have soon learned it was more acceptable to be called Portuguese than Spanish under the rapidly increasing British influence in Spanish La Florida. To this day, many residents of Hancock County, Tennessee, who abhor the racial connotations of the word Melungeon refer to their ancestors as "Portugee." Early census reports of the area occasionally reported individuals as Portuguese. The Portuguese designation following a name was always lined through and mulatto or f.c. (free colored) was usually the final racial description recorded.

After De Soto came a period of non-exploitive inactivity on the continent, the French became interested in new explorations and opportunities. Jean Ribault sailed from France with Lutheran and Calvinistic inclinations toward Catholic La Florida. He passed the Spanish place called Santa Elena, established by the earlier pioneer, Allyson. Ribault and company built their own fort in the same general area and call it Charlesfort. The enclosure was manned by 30 men prior to Ribault's departure for France. Ribault sailed and landed back in France shocked to find his home port under siege by a Catholic army. He, in turn, fled to England to convince Queen Elizabeth of his Protestantism and desire to gain a foothold in La Florida. She concurred, but he suspected her motives were for England and tried to flee, but was thrown into the Tower of London.

Details of the attempted survival of Charlesfort are fascinating. One person remains noteworthy, Guillaume Rouffi, as we move forward with their demise and subsequent launch of a small boat, which eventually lands in England instead of France, with few survivors. The leader of the small boat, Barre, was thrown into the Tower of London, and perhaps he was reunited with Ribault.

In 1563, chaos subsided briefly enough for France to consider sending 300 men and four women aboard three ships to Charlesfort. Coincidentally, Prince Phillip of Spain decided to eliminate Charlesfort from La Florida. A ship with 25 men was dispatched from Spanish Havana toward Charlesfort. Carolina Indians met the Spanish ship with Guillaume Rouffi as guide. Charlesfort was burned, and the Spanish departed, convinced Charlesfort was eliminated. A few days later, the three ships from France arrived in the area to reinforce Charlesfort, and finding it burned, went upstream to build a new Fort Caroline.

By winter, discontent and resource shortages plagued them, yet another small group trying to establish a foothold in the wilderness of North America. First, 13 rebels fled by boat for Cuba. They seized a Spanish ship and reminded the Spanish that the French were still in La Florida. Shortly, another 66 mutinied Fort Caroline, took a ship, and sailed for the Antilles.

Finally in August, four possible relief ships were sighted off-shore, but to the dismay of those in the fort, were flying the English flag. The ships were commanded by John Hawkins and were prowling the rivers and coves for Spanish bounty. They were guided by one of the rebels from Fort Caroline, who had been picked up in the Caribbean. Trading ensued between the ships and the fort for guns and powder, etc. Hawkins departed, and the remaining survivors of the fort waited for the prevailing winds, in order to expeditite their own departure to France. Winds were not accommodating for days, and suddenly, seven new ships appeared on the horizon from the mother country, France. The fleet was commanded by none other than Ribault, who had escaped from the Tower of London and was sent by France to regain a new foothold in La Florida.

The saga continued as the Spanish sent Pedro Menendez from Spain with 18 ships and 1,504 soldiers toward North America, to rid La Florida of the French once and for all. Menendez encountered a hurricane, and his fleet was scattered. He eventually made landfall at Cape Canaveral with only five ships and 600 people, including 26 women. He then sailed northward to reach the area of Fort Caroline by September 4. The newly arrived French ships under the command of Ribault were still riding at anchor off the St. Johns. A minor confrontation ensued before dark, the French fled to sea, and the Spanish went south to dock at a harbor inhabited by natives. Menendez went ashore with banners, trumpets, and great fanfare. Thus, St. Augustine, the oldest permanent settlement in the United States, was established as a result of his conquest on September 8, 1565.

Meanwhile, Ribault at Fort Caroline sailed south toward Menendez, with 12 ships and 600 men, to destroy the Spaniards and their hope for stability in America. The French were caught up in yet another storm as they bore down on Florida, approaching the biggest Spanish warship in the area. The French became totally disoriented off the coast, and, as Menendez recognized their problems, he countered by heading north overland with 500 armed soldiers toward Fort Caroline. Menendez and his men attacked the undefended fort at dawn with the cry of "Santiago." He renamed the fort

Pedro Menendez & Descendant.
Courtesy of National Geographic.

San Mateo. There were a recorded 45 escapees of the slaughter who boarded small ships in the harbor for France. Perhaps some fled to the woods never to be found.

The remnants of Ribault's fleet eventually reached the shore near Cape Canaveral and walked the beaches northward in search of home, Fort Caroline. At dawn on September 29, 1565, the wandering 200 French met the Spanish. The French were put to the knife in groups of ten, with only a dozen who professed Catholicism spared. Ribault's turn came on October 11, as he was intercepted by another group of wanderers to face Menendez on the beach. Ribault offered a huge ransom, but his demise was guaranteed.

Early in 1566, Menendez and a small fleet sailed northward from St. Augustine, mingling with tribes along the route toward the harbor of the original Charlesfort. Here on Parris Island, he built Santa Elena, the center of his new, vast domain and a possible source of the Melungeon origins.

These details of De Soto and the introduction of the second theory of Melungeons who arose from the perils of Santa Elena are necessary as we try to simplify our complex history. The first theory of De Soto and lost men has many details, conjectures, partial facts, flaws, and loopholes that are missing and lost forever. Both laymen and historians tend to select certain popular views that eventually become better known and accepted. In the period after De Soto and prior to Santa Elena, the New World was treacherous and unknown to the many new adventurers. Though they disappeared in great numbers on the new continent, several could have survived to form new, scattered, racial isolates, different looking than their eventual British conquerors. Throughout the entire period there were many early boats dispatched with few or no women, and the human necessity of reproduction knows no racial boundaries in such a situation.

In July of 1567, Juan Pardo, with 250 men, arrived at Santa Elena from Spain. Pardo and his men built a more substantial fort and planned explorations to be initiated by Menendez.

Menendez, who looked to the interior and envisioned a route to New Spain (Mexico), planned stopovers for the looting of rumored rich mines of gold and silver along the way. On November 30, Pardo and 120 men started westward with a local guide. The guide, of French descent, was none other than Guillaume Rouffi, who had remained at Charlesfort when it was abandoned in 1562. He had been quoted as saying, "I'll take my chance with the Indians." He was now leading a Spanish foray into the bush.

Captain Pardo traveled to several Indian settlements, such as Cofitachequi (Muskogee), and on to the foothills of the Appalachians, where he built a fort and placed it under the command of Sargent Hernando Moyano de Morales. During the following spring, a letter reached Santa Elena stating Moyano was in deep trouble with the chief of a tribe just across the mountain. Naturally, the tribe was the Yuchi, who keep recurring in our search for the Melungeons. The chief threatened to eat both Moyano and his dog. Moyano surprised the Yuchi, stormed their village, torched every-

Juan Pardo. Courtesy of National Geographic

thing, and killed 1,000 residents.

After the fight, Moyano took his troops down the Nolichucky River to a town called Chiaha, home of the Chiaha Indians, who spoke the Muskhogean tongue. There has been some confusion in the Pardo translations of exactly where this town was located. For the purpose of our story, it is only important that Juan Pardo secured peace with their 3,000 warriors and proceeded to the village of the main chief. He successfully built another fort in the area.

By September 1567, Pardo had left Santa Elena for another foray into the wilderness. Recent scholars have translated the actual narratives written at Santa Elena in 1569 of this expedition by Pardo. The translations have clarified many of the routes of his predecessor, Hernando De Soto.[13] Captain Pardo traveled the same general areas as De Soto had 27 years earlier. He reached Tanasqui, a town on the Hiwassee, identified by De Soto then went on to the town of the Chiahia Indians. De Soto was also traced by ethnologists to the Tennessee River and the town of the Chiahia. Names have changed and locations are vague, but logic, experience, and nationality, as well as the newest 1979 translation, lead scholars to believe many parts of their routes were the same.[14]

Pardo reached Joara (De Soto called it Xuala) on September 24 and proceeded on toward what is now Asheville, North Carolina. By October 6, he was near Newport, Tennessee. He mentioned passing through the towns of Chalahume and Satapo before hearing of a possible ambush by Indians. He rapidly retreated and found another way to Chiaha. Translations of the names of Chalahume and Satapo survive today, and scholars have been able to identify them as being near Knoxville, Tennessee. As Pardo retraced his route toward home, he built several small, manned forts over the entire route back to Santa Elena in South Carolina. He returned to Santa Elena on March 2, 1568, with badly needed supplies from the natives and tales of the great potential of the frontier.

By 1569, another 193 immigrants arrived with families, to bring the Santa Elena population up to 327 citizens clustered around the fort in 40 small and crowded houses.

The colony almost faltered during this year, as the surrounding small fields and poor soil barely sustained them. They subsisted on oysters and roots until a relief ship arrived.

In 1571, Menendez returned to strengthen the settlement with his leadership. He was accompanied by his wife and a new governor. His canopy bed, carpets, a table service of pewter for 36, and other unnecessary items were symbolic of his planned permanence. The simultaneous occurrence of widespread typhus within the colony neutralized their newest dreams, although the colony rebounded and eventually flourished. The people soon learned that corn, melon, and squash grew well in the area. They learned to export sarsaparilla root, cedar, and oak to Spain.

The colony dreamed of more fertile lands and studied the Juan Vespucci map of 1521. The map detailed the Bay of the Mother of the Gods (Chesapeake) to the north and rekindled their hopes of a route to the Pacific. Good luck provided a local guide in their midst with knowledge of the northern area. In 1561, the Spanish had captured the son of an Indian chief and he was taken to New Spain (Mexico), where the Viceroy recognized him as Don Luis de Velasco. The king eventually sent him home to work as an interpreter and to serve as a native example of converts for the Jesuits. With Don Luis as a guide, the Jesuits, under the leadership of Juan Bautista de Segura, and a young tailor's son called Alfonso who was to assist in mass, embarked toward the north, encountering storms around Capes Fear and Hatteras and the Chesapeake Bay on September 10.

They were in awe as they witnessed the best and largest new port in the world. They crossed the bay and sailed up College Creek. They had no idea that in just 37 years, an island five miles upriver from this bay would be the site the English would call Jamestown.

The Jesuits sailed the five miles of the creek that was navigable to disembark at what is present-day Williamsburg. Along the route, natives on shore recognized the long-lost Don Luis and cheered with joy at the return of one of their own people. The priests portaged their goods over the Williamsburg site, canoed King's Creek to the York River, and built a small church of timber and thatch. Within a week, the converted Don Luis had disappeared on a foray whose purpose was to collect chestnuts and save souls in a village of an uncle. Jesuit Segura's discriminatory opinion was that he was gathering many wives instead of many chestnuts.

By February, the Jesuits had weakened, Segura was ill, and a desperate group was sent out to seek the help of Don Luis in his village. Don Luis was receptive and offered to accompany the priests back to their homes. All three were killed enroute. Don Luis and the warriors returned to the mission in February to obtain trade axes under the pretext of cutting firewood for the priests. He attacked the priests on the spot and killed all except young Alfonso, who was saved by a brother of Don Luis.

By summer, a relief ship finally approached the area of the

Oristas Save Alfonso. Courtesy National Geographic

Jesuits and awaited a safety signal from Segura. Indians costumed as the Jesuits waited boldly on shore for the surprise attack. A skirmish followed, with only two Indians captured, and then the ship fled, sailing southward toward Havana. The Spanish interrogated their captives and learned that one of their own, Alfonso, was still alive in the area of the abandoned mission.

It was over a year later, in August of 1572, when Menendez launched a small expedition of 30 soldiers to attack the Indians at College Creek. The Indians, under siege, produced Alfonso, clothed in a loincloth. Alfonso knelt in subservience at the feet of a priest and struggled to remember his Spanish.

Menendez brought those captured aboard ship, hanged eight or nine for murdering his missionaries, and released the rest to spread the word of his strength and power. Don Luis was not among those captured. Menendez sailed for Spain with plans to return to search for Don Luis. Menendez died two years later in Spain prior to departure with a new fleet.

Historian Carl Bridenbaugh has good circumstantial evidence that Don Luis was actually Opechancanough (he whose soul is white), brother of Powhatan. Powhatan is known for the uprisings of 1622 and 1644 that almost devastated the British colony of Jamestown and will be discussed in the next chapter on Roanoke.

After Menendez's death, the feared uprisings of the Indians began to occur up and down the East Coast. In 1576, the Guale tribe killed one of their own chiefs who had been baptized by the Spanish. Captain Alonso de Solis and his Spanish religious zealots retaliated by departing from Santa Elena to the Guale village, killing two chiefs and cutting the ears off a third. The Guale then captured a Spanish ship off Sapelo Island and killed all those on board the ship.

The Orista tribe, who were in closer proximity to Santa Elena, soon joined the fracas after a small party of Spanish stole their corn. The Indians retaliated before dawn, killing many; among those were Moyano, hero of the demise of 1000 Yuchi and Alfonso, the Jesuit alter boy who survived the ill-fated Chesapeake mission. Only one survived to spread the word of disaster to Santa Elena. The Indians took the offensive, and the settlers at Santa Elena rushed to the creek and boarded boats in haste for their lives, sailing toward St. Augustine. Ten years of hard work and strife were suddenly nothing but billowing smoke on the horizon.

The king of Spain was not to be denied and selected Pedro Menendez Marques, nephew of Pedro Menendez de Aviles to restore stability to La Florida. Marques loaded supplies at St. Augustine and sailed for Santa Elena with vengeance as a goal. The new conquerors burned 19 Guale towns and defeated 300 Oristas armed with bows and arrows. By 1580, the Spanish were again dominant in the area, and 60 homes, a new governor, and 80 men were settled near what was now called the San Marcos Fort.

By this time, the English again pondered a move toward North America. The Queen of England, who had listened to Ribault twenty years before, was now more mature and had a large fleet of privateers at her disposal. By 1584, her own Sir Walter Raleigh was at Cape Hatteras, and the next year Sir Richard Grenville was erecting a fort on Roanoke Island. In 1586, Sir Francis Drake was commanded to go abroad with 42 vessels and 2000 men to pillage La Florida. He first ransacked the main cities of Santo Domingo and Cartagena, then passed Santa Elena and stopped at Roanoke to gather the miserable survivors of the first British attempt to colonize North America. The word of his Spanish conquests spread, and the Santa Elena colonists were ordered to depart for St. Augustine. Santa Elena was forever eliminated from Spanish plans for expansion.

More than 50 thriving Spanish missions remained scattered along the Atlantic seaboard after the demise of Santa Elena. The mission on St. Catherine's Island survived until 1680 when 300 English-led Yamasee Indians drove the Spanish back to St. Augustine. The site has been identified and excavated by archaeologists, and the skeletons of 430 Indian converts have been identified (pages 100-101).

Archaeologists and historians continue to find important artifacts from the settlement of Santa Elena. Numerous forts and other remnants are still being identified and explored.

Many documents and letters of Juan Pardo are signed Joao, which is Portuguese for the Spanish Juan. Pardo was known to be from North Spain, the longtime home of the earlier Moor/Berbers, which shows how complex the issue of Melungeon origin has

Parris Island-Santa Elena. Courtesy of David Brill, National Georgraphic

become at this late date in the history of North America.

Language could be addressed in more detail. Many people have compared current Melungeon names with similar names in Spanish/Portuguese. The word comparisons seem valid, as did earlier Mandan word comparisons with the Welsh and Prince Madoc. We would certainly need to exercise caution due to the similarities of many words in many languages throughout the world.

We have covered the De Soto and Pardo theories in more detail, as they are the more known and accepted theories. However, many other Spanish/Portuguese adventurers might have been the origi-

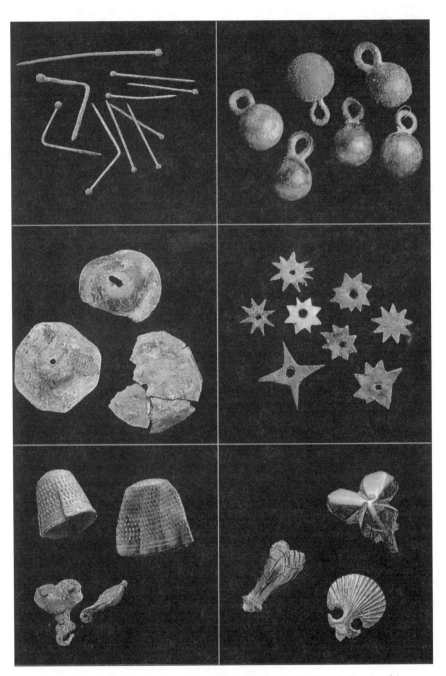

Santa Elena Artifacts. Courtesy Bill Ballenburg, National Geographic.

Portuguese Caravel
Courtesy of Byron Longman

nal descendants of the first Melungeons. The Portuguese were a great sea power in the 1400s and wrote of their many successes in this era. Their ships and their sailors were considered excellent during this period. They were the first known people to have discovered the Madeira Islands in 1419. In 1420, Prince Henry the Navigator established a center for exploration on Cape St. Vincent. In 1434, Gil Eanes rounded Cape Bojador, and in 1441, Antao Goncalves brought the first cargo of slaves and gold from West Africa to Portugal.

They developed better ships with their creation of the sleek, lateen-rigged caravel, which could sail up to five different points on the winds. They perfected the astrolabe, which allowed them to return to a specific spot once its latitude was determined. Skilled mariners sent many different ships out into the Atlantic over the entire period prior to 1500.

The Azores were eventually all discovered and populated with shiploads of Portuguese citizens from the mainland, who were assisted by some Flemings. These islands proved productive to the growth of corn, cattle, and wine, which motivated the seamen toward further exploration. They eventually claimed the first discovery of America by Joao Vaz Corte Real in 1472. After hearing of the Christopher Columbus voyage in 1492, most scholars feel the Portuguese were not able to unlock the secrets of the correct trade winds flowing toward North America prior to 1500.[15] Their logic for the late announcement of being the first to discover America was their supposed secret attempt to claim the entire continental area and possible spoils for themselves.

After 1500, the Portuguese Duke of Braganza led his fleet in a revolt against Spain in 1655, and his landing somewhere on the Eastern Shore was often quoted as a source of a theoretical shipwreck of the first Melungeons. The duke's plan was to reclaim Cuba

Composition	Corrected MMD and SD	Reference
English, 82%; Black, 18%	0.019±0.016	1969
Portuguese, 90%; Cherokee, Black, 5% each	0.022±0.016	1969
Portuguese alone	0.024±0.022	
Portuguese, 94%; Cherokee, 6%	0.027±0.020	1969
Portuguese, 90%; Cherokee, 10%	0.028±0.026	1972
English, 94%; Black, 6%	0.029±0.025	1969
U.S. Whites	0.036±0.034	
U.S. Whites, 90%; Cherokee, 10%	0.043±0.041	1972

Melungeons vs Hybrids. Courtesy of Pollitzer and Brown.

and Florida from the Spaniards. The fleet was never heard of again.[16] Melungeons of today accept the story of the Duke of Braganza, and similar stories, as their tradition of shipwrecked or mutineered Portuguese sailors coming ashore in North Carolina. The stories told of his fleeing men eventually moving farther inland to avoid the law and conflicts with others near the coast. Oral tradition had them living and surviving in harmony with local indigenous people.

It seems pertinent to conclude this chapter with a revisit to some of the genetic possibilities of the Melungeons, which were the subject of studies started by Pollitzer and Brown in the 1960s, and expanded by James Guthrie in 1990. Pollitzer and Brown favored predominately Portuguese ancestry over English for the Melungeons. Guthrie considered newer procedures and concluded an English match was better, but a considerable black percentage was necessary for the mean measure of divergence (MMD) to fit the Melungeon sample.

This chapter shows that many events favor the Spanish/Portuguese ancestry. Many ships traversed back and forth to the Iberian Peninsula during the early period. Shipwrecks, piracy, slave trading, and mutinies resulting in missing or lost people were all an integral part of the pioneering culture. The empire of La Florida was vast, and the people of this Spanish empire explored and exploited everything for gain or religion. Confirming artifacts have been found over a large part of the explored area, and Melungeons even today speak favorably of their "Portugee" ancestry. Some of these early pioneer people of Spain, Portugal, and France must have been lost and survived on the frontier all during this period.

[1]P.R. Collier & Son Encyclopedia, Collier Publishing Company, New York, 1955, Volume 9, pp. 16-18.

[2]Ibid

[3]Joseph Judge, "Exploring Our Forgotten Century," National Geographic, Washington D. C., Volume 173, Number 3, March 1988.

[4]Samuel Cole Williams, *Dawn of the Tennessee Valley and Tennessee History*, The Watauga Press, Johnson City, Tennessee, 1937, p. 4.

[5]Kenneth Freder, *Frauds, Myths, and Mysteries*, Mayfield Publishing Company, Mountain View, California, 1990, p. 100.

[6]Ibid

[7]John R. Swanton, *The Indian Tibes of North America*, Smithsonian Institute Press, Washington, 1952, p. 117.

[8]Dana Olson, *Prince Madoc: Founder of Clark County, Indiana*, Jeffersonville, Indiana, 1987, p. 50.

[9]Ibid

[10]Bonnie Ball, *The Melungeons*, The Overmountain Press, Johnson City, Tennessee, 1992, p. 35.

[11]Jean Patterson Bible, *Melungeons Yesterday And Today*, East Tennessee Printing Company, Rogersville, Tennessee, 1975, p. 95.

[12]Ibid

[13]Joseph Judge, "Exploring Our Forgotten Century," National Geographic, Washington D. C., March 1988, Volume 173, Number 3.

[14]Samuel Cole Williams, p. 5.

[15]Samuel Eliot Morison, "The European Discovery of America," Oxford University Press, New York,1971, pp. 94-105.

[16]James Aswell, "Lost Tribes of Tennessee's Mountains." *Nashville Banner*, August 22, 1937.

Chapter 8
Lost Colony

In the mystery of the origin of the Melungeons, it is natural to move forward in history to the next early period after Santa Elena. In the general area, twenty-seven years later, a small British colony was established on Roanoke Island.

How did the idea evolve for the first British colony? It is valuable to observe some selected details in the process of the establishment and settlement of Roanoke. These details will help us to be aware of the complexities involved in our search for the origin of the elusive Melungeons.

The failure of Charlesfort in 1562 and, later, Fort Caroline in 1564 strained the French enthusiasm for colonies in the New World. Meanwhile, in England, a new curiosity was developing for the distant lands across the Atlantic. Sir Humphry Gilbert was foremost among those Englishmen who dreamed of rising up against the mighty seapower of Spain. Sir Humphry was a student of navigation and the sea, with the added benefit of having a strong knowledge of the principals of military science. In 1577, he communicated to Queen Elizabeth his bold plan to outfit a fleet of warships under the pretext of exploration to the New World. His real

Sir Humphry Gilbert
Courtesy of Ivor Noel Hume

scheme was to loot the Spanish. He planned to intercept as many Spanish ships as possible, reducing their profitable, established trade with Newfoundland and the West Indies.

By this time, the queen was thirty-three years old and fifteen years into her long reign. She had gained wisdom over the years and did not feel the timing was right for Gilbert's plan without a declaration of war.

By June 1578, the queen had reconsidered and consented by charter for Gilbert to "discover, search, find out, and view such remote heathen and barbarous lands, countries, and territories, not actually possessed of any Christian Prince or people."

The bold and dangerous plan of 1577 to attack and disrupt Spanish shipping lanes was now more sudued. Gilbert was expected to establish an English settlement as a base of operations a distance from Spanish Florida.

Who became the fleet leader of such an idea for an English colony? Popular history jumps to Walter Raleigh, but originally Simon Ferdinando was the designated captain of all the ships of the fleet. Simon Ferdinando was of Portuguese descent, being born and named Simao Fernandes on the island of Terceira in the Azores. Formerly, he had trained as a ship's pilot before switching his allegience to Spain to be renamed the Spanish equivalent of Simon Fernandez.

During his Spanish period, he made at least one trip across the Atlantic to North America. He had investigated the coast above Florida and the Outer Banks during his tenure from 1561-1573 with Spain. He is credited as the first to reach the sounds of North Carolina from the Atlantic, and his name frequented early English maps as Port Ferdinando.

During his Spanish tour of duty, he turned against Spain and became a pirate, roaming the coasts in search of bounty. He was not selective as to who he looted and even turned up in port with a ship of Dutch registry. He captured Portuguese vessels on two occassions. The first was successful, but the second was a bit bloody, with the Portuguese ambassador objecting to numerous killings aboard the ship. He reported seven killed personally by Ferdinando and demanded Ferdinando be hanged. The queen had to respond, and Ferdinando was jailed. The wild event caught the attention of prominant persons in England, who began to recognize the advantage of having such an experienced navigator to exploit the shipping routes of Spain in the West Indies.

Ferdinando had to be charged with piracy to appease the ambassador of Portugual, and he was charged with suspicion of piracy, and then, suddenly, the charges were dropped. At almost the same time, he entered the service of Sir Francis Walsingham, the secretary of state and a strong advocate of England's explorations across the sea. Walsingham had the vision and the power to manipulate and initiate the idea of an English presence in the New World.

Sir Humphry Gilbert was now ready to fulfill his charter of 1578 to work the new lands. He had a capable crew leader in the presence of the very experienced and ruthless pirate, Simon Ferdinando. Gilbert's next step was to gather ten ships, under the auspices of the queen, with his half-brother Walter Raleigh in command. The lead ship was the 100-ton *Falcon,* with the young Raleigh alongside the pilot and master, Simon Ferdinando.

Raleigh, a soldier, and Ferdinando, a pirate, were not compatible, and the fleet did not depart before November of 1578. During the delay, all ships but the *Falcon* became preoccupied with local pirating activities. By the time they finally departed, all the other ships detoured and turned in at Ireland for repairs and supplies. The *Falcon* proceeded alone to the Canaries and the Cape Verde Islands. By the summer of 1579, Raleigh and Ferdinando aborted the mission across the Atlantic and turned around to return to England, thus, aborting the first dreams of the colony of Roanoke.

Gilbert remained optimistic in spite of the failed first attempt and planned a more conservative second effort to establish a foothold in America. This time he decided to send his own small frigate of less than ten tons, the *Squirrel,* to search for a colony site. Gilbert, once again, decided to depend upon the Portuguese Ferdinando to expedite and assure the search. Ferdinando departed in March of 1580 with only ten men to explore a considereable portion of New England, and he was back in England in rapid fashion to report on possible sites to colonize. The rapid dispatch and return of the ship was to please and impress those involved with invested monies. The quick trip also attemped to prove that Ferdinando was very focused and stayed with his assignments. It assured the

Left: Dr. John Dee in a 1792 engraving. *Right:* Martin Frobisher, reengraved in 1849 from a 1620 original.

Dee & Frobisher. Courtesy of Ivor Noel Hume.

investors that he could ignore all the great opportunities to pursue his favorite vocation of looting.

Gilbert planned for another foray to the New World after the return of Ferdinando, but as time slipped by, Ferdinando diviated off into other projects. He first worked with Dr. John Dee, the mathmatician, astrologer, alchemist, and geographer. He supplied Dr. Dee with a sea chart of the Atlantic.

Ferdinando also worked with Captain Martin Frobisher of the Muscovy Company. His role was to advise the outfitting of ships by Frobisher for a precious metal search in Newfoundland. Frobisher eventually made a round trip and returned with a hold of ore which, upon scientific analysis, proved worthless. After this ill-fated voyage, Ferdinando returned to his true vocation of privateering.

In 1582, Gilbert was ready for an excursion to the New World without Ferdinando, who had hired on as a copilot to China. Gilbert prepared this excursion with a broader range of legal powers. He was authorized to carry out and enforce laws as he saw fit.

He even deeded portions of land that have never been seen in the country across the Atlantic. The parcels ranged from a few hundred acres to one parcel of two million acres.

His fleet was composed of five vessels ranging in size from the less than ten-ton *Squirrel*, which had crossed earlier with Ferdinando, to the two-hundred ton *Raleigh*, owned by Walter Raleigh. Gilbert's lack of organizational skills without Ferdinando delayed the loading and departure of 260 men until late fall of 1582. Eventually, bad weather on the North Atlantic foiled the attempt and the mission was aborted until the early summer of 1583.

They followed the northern trade winds and arrived near Newfoundland instead of further south as had been planned. The area was alive with fisherman who had been fishing the area for several decades. Upon arrival, Gilbert counted at least thirty-six vessels in the immediate area. The ships represented the nations of Spain, Portugual, France, and Britian.

The summer fishermen of these many countries had a rudimentary form of government. The first arrivals each spring established headquarters on shore. During any dispute, equal representatives of each country ruled on the problem. Crops were planted by various fishermen along the coast to supplement semi-wild cattle that the Portuguese had released many years before. Over the years, the cattle had multiplied, providing a variety of protein to the many fishermens' diets.

Gilbert spent time ashore to plant his flag of England with pomp and circumstance, just as John Cabot had done more than 80 years earlier. He decided against a permanent base as two of his five ships had been lost at sea, and the fall season had arrived, hampering the seasonal efforts of the crew. He departed after a short time with his three remaining ships and cruised the nearby islands prior to departure. To his dismay, another storm hit the ships with him riding the stern on the smaller *Squirrel* to disaster. All hands were lost.

During the winter of 1583-84, the heirs of Gilbert in England scurried to attempt another voyage and colony before the expiration of their charter by Queen Elizabeth. They were unable to present a plan, and on March 25, 1584, Walter Raleigh, half-brother of Gilbert, came forward to receive a new charter similar to the earlier charter of the area of Newfoundland. He was to explore the "remote heathen and barbarous Lands, Countries, and territories."[1] A new charter bestowed upon Raleigh, as Gilbert before him, the right to deed lands as yet unseen to willing settlers in his adventure. Ordinary participants in the endeavor would receive 500 acres and more responsible persons much more. Raleigh retained many mining rights and other facets of the new empire that might benefit his needs. Of course, all of this unknown land was inhabited by Native Americans.

As we begin to envision the complexities of a future Roanoke, we can perceive the problems involved in later identifying any pockets of non-British settlers that might be precursors to Melungeons. Many people had already reached the New World over many years. We ask again, did any of these people stay, or were any abandoned or shipwrecked? Did any procreate with the Spanish, French, or other survivors from other nations? Were slave genes involved in some of the eventual survivors? Did any eventually mix with indigenous people or some of the tribes mentioned in association with Melungeons (Yuchi, Mandan, Saponi, Powhatan)? We see that the new coastal area was described as "crawling" with boats of foreigners of many nations as early as 1583. This had been the situation for several decades.

Raleigh attempted to establish a colony in the New World, and he sent another reconnaissance mission across the Atlantic on April 27, 1584. A two-vessel fleet departed with Master Philip Amadas in charge and Master Arthur Barlowe behind in a smaller ship. Barlowe was in charge of records for Walter Raleigh. By this time, Simon Ferdinando returned to lead the foray into the new lands. Ferdinando knew the sea, and this time he avoided a landfall in Newfoundland by going south toward the West Indies. By June 10, they were in the heart of Spanish territory somewhere in the West Indies. They took on food and water and headed north toward the Carolinas, while avoiding the ever-present Spanish in their own domain. By July 4, they were in sight of what is now the Carolina coast. Ferdinando proved his extensive skills as a helmsman by spending nine days and 120 miles cautiously cruising along the often shifting sand shoals for a safe entrance to Port Ferdinando.

After waiting at anchor for a full two days, Barlowe and Amadas approached the shore in a small boat with seven fellow crewmen.

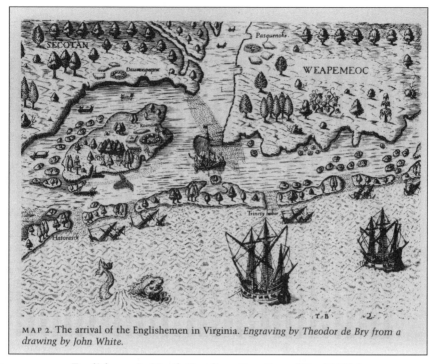

MAP 2. The arrival of the Englishemen in Virginia. *Engraving by Theodor de Bry from a drawing by John White.*

Englishmen In North Carolina. Courtesy of David Stick.

Standing on the shore was a lone Indian patiently waiting for their arrival. Granganimeo, brother of chief Wingina, appeared to be amiable and friendly. He made all sorts of gestures of welcome prior to offering trade objects and gifts for the new visitors. Eventually, the small crew was transported twenty miles up the coast to the village for more festivities and cultural exchanges. The strangers were surrounded by maidens of Granganimeo's wife, who removed their clothing in preparation for washing the crew members. The welcome washing concluded with all the shipmen's feet being washed separately by the maidens in warm water. By evening, the members of the expedition were more relaxed, but still chose to sleep offshore in their small boat, much to the dismay of the new hosts. During the night it rained in the bay, and the people on shore paddled into the bay with "fine matts to cover them from the rayne." The next night the natives once again tried to convince the men to come ashore, but the importance of the mission caused them to be very cautious. Barlowe responded with, "certainly there was no cause of doubt; for a more kinde and loving people, there can not be found in the world, as farre as we have hitherto had triall."

The crew spent a period on shore in harmony with their new hosts. They were even invited to participate in a combined surprise attack on a nearby Neiosioke town. Their new guns and metal weapons were impressive to the local warriors. They refused to be a part of any battles as they were, "uncertain whether their per-swasion be to the ende they may be revenged of their enemies, or for the love they beare to us."

The Indians of Wingandacon were as impressed with the white-ness of the skin of the newcomers as with their guns, but they had seen white people before. They told of shipwrecked sailors near Pamlico some twenty years before who were rescued. At that time, canoes were strapped together and the survivors tied shirts together for sails. The men departed in the makeshift boat to never be seen again. The abandoned boats were found later near other islands. Perhaps all were lost to the sea.

Amadas and Barlowe had gathered specimens and prepared to depart for Britian. The Indians expressed their ultimate trust as they allowed two of their own, Mateo and Wanchese, to accompany the voyage back across the sea.[2]

These first natives contacted were called the Wingandacon by Barlowe and Amadas, but now seem to have been the tribe of the Machapunga or Pamlico, who eventually united with other tribes in the Tuscarora War. The last remnants of the Machapunga were noted in 1761 by the Reverend Alex Stewart from North Carolina as he babtized seven with mixed-blood children. By this late date, only 7 or 8 warriors were reported left in this tribe of 1200 strong at the time of Barlowe and Amadas.

The Palmlico tribe was probably called the Wingandacon, because they were decimated when 1,000 members were lost to smallpox in 1696, and after the Tuscarora War, they were ordered totally destroyed to satisfy a treaty made between those Indians loyal to the British. The balance of the Palmico was enslaved by the Indian loyalists.[3]

Simon Ferdinando made another quick and uneventful return trip across the Atlantic with the Amadas and Barlowe vessels to reach England in mid-September. Details were already being collected to convince Queen Elizabeth to continue providing influence and funds for Roanoke. Richard Hakluyt, an ordained minister skilled in geography and exploration, prepared a discourse based on more than random sailing. He had studied the entire situation to formulate a plan that he felt would assure success in the New World.

His basic premise was the need to wrest a share of the monopoly of trade and treasure from Spain. His checklists of materials needed for success and shipment were extensive, as were his reasons for the endeavor. He advocated the adventure as a means to increase power for the queen, fill the royal coffers, and counter the Catholicism of the Spanish with Protestanism. The basic ideas were appealing, as England was in recession, unemployment was high, and even the numbers and care of orphans was uncontrollable. He proposed employment for veterans who would guard the colonists and the release of many prisoners and orphans to provide a workforce. Ships could be built in the new colony, with the plentiful source of wood, and be manned with local labor for both trade and war.

Hakluyt's expertise in the ministry shone as he discussed the need to convert savages to Protestantism and cause the Indians to "revolte cleane from the Spaniarde." He felt the new enlightenment and satisfaction of finding the God of the Protestants would stabilize them and provide a buffer for a stronger Roanoke against the Spanish. Lastly, Hakluyt spoke of a base of operations closer to an unknown passage to the Orient, which was still felt to be somewhere through or around the new continent.

By the spring of 1585, the discourse of Hakluyt had passed all legal channels, and Walter Raleigh had procured Sir Richard Grenville to command a fleet of seven vessels. Captain Ralph Lane, a military expert, was to assist the experienced Portuguese pilot, Simon Ferdinando.

The queen remained a bit leery of the entire plan, but approved of a change in name of the colony from Wingandacon to Virginia, in honor of herself, the Virgin Queen of England. She also responded by knighting Raleigh, to Sir Walter Raleigh, and providing a large flagship, the *Tiger*, with a bonus of access to the stocks of the royal gunpowder.

Sir Richard Grenville. Courtesy of David Stick.

By April of 1585, the fleet finally departed from Plymouth with Grenville aboard the *Tiger*, Amadas as admiral and second in command, and Barlowe in a lesser role. After leaving west out of the Canaries, a storm hit to scatter the fleet. The *Tiger* reached the Leewards by May 7 without a tender and sailed northward to what is believed to be present-day Puerto Rico and the "Baye of Muskito." Grenville pondered the fate of the other ships as he anchored in the heart of Spanish waters. Finally, Ralph Lane was sent ashore to secure the area with workers and soldiers. The plan was to build a sea going escort for the *Tiger*.

As luck would have it, the nearby Spanish garrison was weakened by demands in other areas. After four days of activity, the English spotted a few Spanish on horseback observing the construction of the boat, but they fled without any confrontation.

By May 19, men aboard the *Tiger* saw masts on the horizon and recognized one of their missing fleet. All the other ships were still missing as Grenville and his locally built pinnace departed with the newly arrived *Elizabeth*. Optimism improved as Grenville captured a Spanish frigate the first day out and another the second day, with a bonus of a bountiful cargo. Lane and the troops also went ashore during this period to secure necessary salt from a known Spanish saltworks. They were able to loot the area and return to ship before Spanish reinforcements could be summoned.

Onward to Hispaniola, Grenville anchored with his five ships in the port of Isabela. He blew tumpets and put up such a facade that the Spanish, with an entourage of servants and Negroes, greeted him as royalty, enjoyed feasting aboard his ship, hosted games on shore, and arranged gift exchanges. It is assumed the English exchanged their captured Spanish boatmen, because they were willingly supplied with live horses, cattle, sheep, and swine, as well as hides, sugar, ginger, pearls, and tobacco to take toward Virginia.

On June 26, 1585, the small fleet reached the area somewhere near Roanoake. In spite of Ferdinando's expertise and caution, the *Tiger* entered an inlet and went aground. Even today, the underwater shifting sands in the area are treacherous for motor-driven boats and modern navigation equipment. The *Tiger* sank by the 29th, and, as salvage operations were under way, reports circulated of the discovery of thirty men roaming on nearby Croatoan. They were identified as members of one of the other ill-fated ships which dropped them off before going on toward Newfoundland.

It was July 6th before Grenville received a favorable report from the Indian scout, Manteo. He prepared a group to be sent to select the site for a colony. Four small, shallow-draft boats and fifty men with an eight-day supply of provisions were dispatched up the waterways. They visited three Indian villiages, Pomeiooc, Secotan, and Aquascogoc in their explorations, and, as luck would have it, the artist John White was aboard the rear vessel to provide a visual

Town of Pomeiooc. Courtesy of David Stick.

recording of two of the sites.

The spirited explorers spent July and part of August trying to survive and build Fort Raleigh. The relationship of Grenville and Lane deterioriated to the point of destoying the entire concept of British colonization. In one incident, Lane was sent to Cape Rojo for salt, along with twenty-five men and a few Spanish prisoners, with assurances from Grenville that there was no possibility of danger. He was met by forty Spanish horsemen and three hundred foot soldiers. Letters recorded in England tell of Grenville eventually considering a trial and death sentence for Lane and verbalizing accusations against the pilot Ferdinando for incompetence.

Town of Secotan. Courtesy of David Stick.

In spite of the many conflicts, the fort was built by August 25, and Grenville departed for England with 200 of the 300 men available for the colony. Six days out to sea, Grenville encountered a three-hundred ton Spanish ship loaded with cargo and finished the voyage with his captured prize. Ferdinando took control of the *Tiger* and reached England on October 6, twelve days ahead of Grenville, who manned the added Spanish ship.[4]

Raleigh's original plan had been to send supplies and reinforcemnts to arrive in the colony at about the time that Grenville departed for England. King Philip of Spain had other plans. He began to sieze British ships in retaliation for their aid to Protestantism. The king also needed to resupply the granaries of Spain as a result of a crop failure. Unknown to the colony, their scheduled supply ships had been diverted in England and became a part of the Newfoundland fishing fleet.

The continued disruptions and conflicts between the Spanish and British returns us to a name we considered in our Moor/Berber theory of the Melungeons, Sir Francis Drake. These chaotic incidents played into the personality of Drake, who thrived on pirating of any sort.

Drake had tried for years to interest the queen in an attack to conquer New Spain in order to control the shipping and expansion of the Spanish empire. The queen had been afraid she might see the Spanish crossing the channel. The continual seizure of British ships by the Spanish changed her perception of his previous idea.

On September 14, 1585, Drake left Plymouth with twenty-five ships and twenty-three hundred soldiers and mariners. He planned to capture Santo Domingo and Cartagena before going north to the silver mines of Honduras. He looted the Iberian coast on the way, just to fulfill the sheer joy of his vocation and spread the word of his New World endeavor.

His last stop at Sao Tiago for water and supplies seemed uneventful as he organized his troops and torched the town in honor of his departure. Unfortunately, a few days out to sea, the men began to sicken and die. At least 300 died in a short period. In spite of his misfortune, he did attack Cartagena and Santo Domingo with limited financial success, but skipped the silver mines as well as Panama. He couldn't resist a hit on St Augustine before he headed back, and he destoyed Fort San Juan enroute to the looting and burning of St. Augustine. He saved some windows and other building hardware from the colony before he sailed on northward to warn the colonists of the growing Spanish threats throughout the area.

He sailed with a large array of ethnic people that he had freed or looted from the Spanish. These nationalities, enumerated in a previous chapter, complicated Drake's final stop with the colonists. He felt the need to expedite his arrival to the colonists, after leaving England on September 14, 1585, and now in June, 1586, he had just destroyed St. Augustine. He also knew the first supply ships were diverted to the Newfoundland fishing waters and a later supply fleet was sent to the colonists.

On June 11, 1586, Drake and Lane stood face to face. Lane found Drake was not there with needed food supplies, and Drake found that the colony was in bad shape, with no need for additional castoffs. They surmised war with Spain might have been declared by that time, and a second group of ships with food might not have been on the way from England. Compromises were made, and Drake provided some provisions, a ship, and some skilled laborers to allow the colony to survive until the next supply ships appeared on the horizon.

A chaotic sequence of events continued as a storm hit on June 13, and by June 16, the seas had not calmed. Lane had enough and asked for Drake to take his people home. Drake's reluctant sailors rowed ashore in the storm and saved the people, but they allowed no room on the small boats for the colonists' personal belongings. Records are scant; therefore, what happened to some 250 Negroes that Drake had planned to dump, as well as some of the other ethnic peoples who were left behind is not known. Did he leave behind any colonists in his rush to survive the storm? Some say at least three were in the bush and left behind in the frenzy to load in the storm. Such was the mystery of the genetic makeup of the many people on the frontiers of the New World.

A relief ship arrived within days of the colonists' departure, to find no one. The shipmen barely checked the area before heading back toward England with all provisions still aboard. Grenville was close behind with three vessels and 400 men. Why did the first ship leave so quickly? Grenville's delay of another 14 days had been self-imposed by his decision to loot an English ship which he accused of illegal trade with Spain. This manuever supplied him with wine and oil. He then captured two French boats with fine crews which he sent back to England as captured loot. He also captured a Dutch boat bound for Spain. Colonizing seemed to be secondary to pirating!

Grenville was more thorough and sent a a Spanish pilot, Pedro Diaz, and a few others ashore to investigate. They found no one except a hanging white man and Indian, side by side. Who were the strange twosome and why were they executed together? They also captured three Indians and, according to Diaz, one spoke enough English to tell of the colonists leaving with Drake. He may have also told Grenville and his people of the colonists' abuse of every tribe within their range as a negative factor in their fragile existance.[5]

Grenville decided to leave only a few men and departed for England. Perhaps the plentiful food supply coerced the small numbers to stay, but it was more likely the direct commands from Grenville. This small group lasted until two Indian decoys turned up to secure entrance, while 28 others remained hidden in the woods. The ambush was successful as the Indians drove the men to the supply house and torched it with fire arrows. The white men fled in boats for their lives. They were never seen or heard from again. This detail was told to John White by a Croatoan Indian in 1587.

The John White expedition of April 26, 1587, under Sir Walter Raleigh's three-year charter, consisted of three ships, but the personnel suddenly had a new look. This time there were English craftsmen, a few educated men, some Welshmen, and a few Irishmen. This expedition of 150 landed in late July, and also included seventeen women and nine children.[6] Now, there was no longer a need for the isolated men to spread their reproductive prowess wherever they could; now, they were starting with a more stable plan of a permanent English colony. This plan proved better, initially, with the first British colonial birth on August 18 of Virginia Dare, born of John White's daughter and Ananias Dare. The girl was named for Virginia, and naturally she is remembered over one born aboard the ship and one shortly after landing called Harvie.

This voyage too started poorly, with Simon Ferdinando wanting to loot and pilliage all enemy ships and John White trying to protect the passengers from danger to ensure an attempt at colonization. Ferdinando had constantly been a problem, as he had always been of a dubious character, but his sailing skills to the New World were impeccable. The small party lost two Irishmen to the Spaniards in a skirmish, but landed basically intact at Lane's Island encampment of the year before.

The fleet's plan was to stop at the colony briefly to check on the 15 men who had been left earlier by Grenville and had arrived too late to reinforce the previous core group. During this brief foray, Ferdinando prematurily dumped all of the new shipment of people.

The original plan was to go northward with these people to the Chesapeake area where better land and other resources were confirmed to be available for survival. The drop-off time was too late for a crop; therefore, the colonists had to depend upon available stores until the next summer. They also expected some generosity from the local Indians, but by this time, the Indians in the area had been abused beyond cooperation even to the extent of having their chief, Wingina, killed the year before by Ralph Lane.[7]

After a very short period, this small group conceded it was necessary to send to England for assistance. Experience had taught them that more people needed to be left behind to insure survival of a long-term plan. Eventually, they determined John White himself needed to return to England to assure a good response from those who could reinforce their group. Those that remained, approximately sixty men with twenty-seven women and children, were chosen to depart northward approximately 50 miles to the Cheasapeake area. They were to settle at what was the site origionally chosen prior to their being dumped by Ferdinando. White left instructions for them to carve the name of any new location on a conspicuous tree and, if in danger, to carve the sign of the Maltese Cross above their location.[8]

White returned to England via Ireland, amid storms and sickness, and arrived on November 8 to find Philip II of Spain massing ships in all the Western ports for a possible invasion of England. Ferdinando's ship had arrived three weeks earlier, but with many sick and dead. He hardly reached home base. Thus ended many joys and sorrows with Ferdinando who Quinn describes as, "violent, quarrelsome, and unattractive, though an able man."

The mighty Spanish Aramada was still building, when White was able to slip two small pinnaces out of the harbour early on April 22, 1588. The usual plan of pirateering ended in disaster. By May 22nd, they were back in port, with a notation by White in his journal, "home into Cornwell within fewe weekes after our arrival, without performing our intended voyage for the reliefe of the planters in Virginia, which thereby were not a little distressed."

Following the defeat of the Spanish Armada in August 1588, no relief was sent to Roanoke through 1589. Unfortunately, the Spanish Armada began to regroup, and England had to again prepare for a possible invasion.

In 1590, in spite of Drake's new fleet of 140 ships and 8,000 soldiers, plans were formulated for three ships to return to the colonists. This time Edward Spicer, a friend of White's, was in charge. White, along with new settlers, was to be included on the passenger lists. On August 17th, the crews reached Hatteras to find violent weather, as one ship went aground, and members tried to wade ashore. Several drowned in the landing attempt.

Finally, they landed to see the first signs of the colonists, as CRO was emblazoned on a prominant tree at the landing site. The seamen progressed farther and found the entire word CROATOAN on a debarked tree at the entrance to Roanoke.[9] This was a puzzling message, because the colonists were to have gone north to the Chesapeake and not south to be with their Indian friend Manteo's Croatoan tribe. By August 18, the men were back aboard the main ships and off for England. Remnants were found, but no sign of people.

The Lost Colony remained alive in the minds of Spaniards, who went to the general area several times over the next few years looking for intruders from England. Until 1603, the colony remained in the fiction and fantasy of England. Raleigh proposed to look for them in 1595, but he was busy with other entrepreneurial activities in Guiana and other locations.

In 1602, Raleigh, fearing the loss of lands from his expired charter, had an experienced mariner by the name of Mace return to look for the Lost Colony. Mace was paid by the month to expedite his trip and attempt to eliminate his desires for privateering. His fleets found nothing of the colony. Eventually, Raleigh lost sight of the entire enterprise, was subsequently charged with treason, convicted, and imprisoned in the Tower of London.

Later, other people told of experiences concerning the Lost Colonists. In 1604, prisoners in St. Augustine who sailed for Englishman John Jerome told of their ship being instructed to stop at Croatoan where Englishmen had settled. They had been instructed to land and trade for the herb, Oyssan or Bissanque, a plant said to have fibers for a type of silk production. The prisoners also told of how their ship lost a sea battle to the Spanish off the coast of South Carolina and that the loss resulted in their incarceration at St. Augustine.[10]

The Powhatan Indians, with a population of 9,000, composed of six tribes plus 24 other groups conquered after the ascension of chief Powhatan, have been frequently mentioned as culprits in the absorption or dissolusion of the Lost Colony.

Opechancanough, the brother of Powhatan and his eventual heir, was previously mentioned as we examined his response to foreign invaders. As we recalled his role, Opechancanough was captured by the Spanish as a youngster in 1561 and was renamed Don Luis de Velasco after visiting Spain and Mexico. We remembered his role of trust and deception of the Spanish. In 1572, Don Luis (Opechancanough) prevailed as the Spaniard Menendez dispached troops and lost in his attempt to rescue missionaries and kill Don Luis at Santa Elena.[11] The hanging of eight Indians in the fiasco and the escape of Opechcanough set the scene for a later hopeful group comprised of Englishmen north of Santa Elena at Roanoke.

Powhatan confessed to Captain John Smith that he had been at the murder of that colony and showed to Captain Smith a musket barrel, and a bronze mortar, and certain pieces of iron which had been theirs.[12] Traditionally, Indians did not kill women and chil-

---

Subdivisions

Subtribes constituting this group are as follows:

Accohanoc, in Accomac and part of Northampton Counties, Va., and probably extending slightly into Maryland.
Accomac, in the southern part of Northampton County, Va.
Appomattoc, in Chesterfield County.
Arrohattoc, in Henrico County.
Chesapeake, in Princess Anne County.
Chickahominy, on Chickahominy River.
Chiskiac, in York County.
Cuttatawomen, in King George County.
Kecoughtan, in Elizabeth City County.
Mattapony on Mattapony River.
Moraughtacund, in Lancaster and Richmond Counties.

Subdivisions of Powhatan. Courtesy of Smithsonian Institute Press.

Mummapacune, on York River.
Nansemond, in Nansemond County.
Nantaughtacund, in Essex and Caroline Counties.
Onawmanient, in Westmoreland County.
Pamunkey, in King William County.
Paspahegh, in Charles City and James City Counties.
Pataunck, on Pamunkey River.
Piankatank, on Piankatank River.
Pissasec, in King George and Westmoreland Counties.
Potomac, in Stafford and King George Counties.
Powhatan, in Henrico County.
Rappahannock, in Richmond County.
Secacawoni, in Northumberland County.
Tauxenent, in Fairfax County.
Warrasqueoc, in Isle of Wight County.
Weanoc, in Charles City County.
Werowocomoco, in Gloucester County.
Wicocomoco, in Northumberland County.
Youghtanund, on Pamunkey River.

Subdivisions of Powhatan. Courtesy of Smithsonian Institute Press.

dren, but perhaps he did kill a large portion of the men and absorbed the women and children, to later become a nucleus of some sort of mixture called Melungeons. Some of the men might have escaped the assault, because considerable time was spent foraging for food items in the bush.

Mr. Jack Goins, researcher for the Goins Foundation, has done extensive research in the area of these Indian people. He has many personal notes and data that suggest Powhatan and the Pomokey Indians were indeed a major nucleus of the original Melungeons.

John Smith figured into many possible theories, as he spent considerable time pondering and searching for the colony. Opechancanough told him of clothed white men being south in a place called Ocanahonan. Smith sent scouts to the general area without maps, because all maps were either inaccurate or nonexistant. The scouts heard reports of white persons but found none. The reports were of whites working in the area of copper mining. Perhaps this is a connection to the Melungeon folklore of mines, metal working, and the counterfeiting of metal coins. This unsolved metal working and mining mystery had already appeared as a motivational factor in the De Soto expeditions, the Yuchi Indians, and now with remnants of the Lost Colony.

Another problem with John Smith's many leads was the known deviousness of Powhatan and brother Opechancancanough. They first spoke of survivors to the south and later confessed to killing all the colonists. These Indian brothers had been abused by the Spanish and now the British, and they were playing a game of survival. Smith, likewise, knew of Powhatan's honorary reception of an insignia by King James, which made him a dependent of the king. The insignia, theoretically, would require the king's permission for any legal action against its recipient. Perhaps Smith learned in the ceremony of 1607 that he had been saved by Powhatan and his daughter, Pocohontas, in order to become a part of Powhatan's inner circle. His relationship with Powhatan may have been a priority. John Smith was proud and ambitious, maybe to the detriment of further searching for the Lost Colonists.[13]

Some theorists feel the Roanoke group split early, and some went south; therefore, the name Croatoan. This tribe was probably erronously called Croatoan but were actually the Hatteras. John Lawson told of the Hatteras Indians having, "white ancestors who could talk in a book as we do; the truth of which is confirmed by grey eyes being found frequently amongst these Indians and no others....It is probable that this Settlement miscarried for want of timely Supplies from England; or through the treachery of the Natives." In 1607, George Percy describes a "Savage boy about the age of ten yeeres, which had a head of haire of a perfect yellow and a reasonable white skin, which is a miracle amongst all Savages."[14]

In 1609, Sir Thomas Gates was told to establish a colony in the south near the Roanoke and Chowan Rivers where nearby were rich copper mines. He was also told of the presence in the area of "four or five English alive, left by Sir Walter Rawley." Gates was told, they live under the protection of a weanoe called Gepanocon, "by whose consent you will never recover them. One of these was worth much labor."[15] Was this an implication they were valuable for their expertise in mining technology?

In the context of the Lost Colony, we should investigate the Lumbees (Indians?), sometimes called the Croatoan of Robeson County, North Carolina, for a brief period. In Robeson County in 1865, the Civil War had caused a degree of lawlessness that allowed looting for hunger, hatred, and revenge for whatever reason came to mind. The wealthier former plantation owners were sometimes robbed at numerous locations on the same night. The Lowery band of Lumbee renegades was suspected in all the crimes that occurred over a nine-year period, even though many were probably committed by other vindictive persons trying to overthrow local wealth and authority.

Henry Berry Lowery was the head of the gang descended from a family of slave owners who were dark and had lost their assets during the Civil War. They were eventually reduced to the status of local Negros, with no rights. This brought out the revenge factor in the Lowery gang, and all proslavery, anti-reconstuction, white, and politically prominant persons were chosen as targets for looting and harrassment. They victimized state senators, governors, bank presidents, and even the sheriff.

Henry Berry Lowery was once ambushed in a boat on Lumbee Creek by the militia of the county and overcame them in a shootout. He retaliated by robbing the safe from both the sheriff's office and a large firm in town. He then left the empty safes in the middle of the street in downtown Lumberton in defiance of their power.

He and his gang were so successful in pillaging, then disappearing to their homes in the swamps that, in desperation, the sheriff arrested four of the gang's wives to use as bait for their surrender. The Loweries responded, "To the Sheriff of Robeson Couty&C. L. Sinclair: We make a request, that our wives who were arrested a few days ago, and placed in Jail, be released to come home to their families by Monday Morning, and if not the Bloodiest times will be here that ever was before—the life of every man will be in Jeopardy. If not we will commence to drench the country in blood and ashes. [Signed]

Henry B. Lowery, Steven Lowery, Andrew Strong, Boss Strong."

The wives were sent home on time with an armed guard to assure their security.[16]

Despite the entire gang being declared outlaws, only one was shot. The rest vanished. Citizens rationalized this attack by assuring themselves only a super human could have affected their lives in such a manner.

Giles Leach, a prominant lawyer of Robeson County, was called to Washington to report on the Ku Klux Klan's activites in his county, with emphasis on the importance of the organization for the stability of the social order. Leach and Mary Norment, whose husband had belonged to the local militia and was killed by the Lowery gang, testified to Lowery's superhuman qualities and racial identity, "Henry Berry Lowery... is of mixed blood, strongly commingled, having coursing in his veins the blood of the Tuscarora Indian, the cavalier blood of England and also that of the descendants of Ham in Africa, his great-great grandmother being a copper-colored negress, raised on the banks of the James River in Virginia...The color of his skin is of a mixed white and yellow, partaking of an admixture, resembling copper however, still predominating, though the white and black remain apparent. Such a skin is affected very little by heat or cold...or by exposure, or good housing...The color of his eyes is a grayish hazel...his hair was straight and black like an Indian's. He is 26 years old, five feet ten inches high, and weighs about one hundred and fifty pounds..."

She continues: "He carries five six-barreled revolvers around his waist with a Henry rifle and sixteen cartridges. In addition... He carries a long-bladed knife and a doubled-barreled shotgun, his whole equipment weighing not less than eighty pounds...With all his armour he could run, swim, stand weeks of exposure in the swamps, walk day and night and take sleep by little snatches, which in a few days would tire out white or negro.

"Occassionally his blood and inclinations will crop out, and his three natures of white, Indian, and negro will come forward and show themselves to the close observer. His Indian nature may be traced by using his mulatto women as an auxiliary to war and plunder. His cavalier (white) scrupulousness may also be observed in the matter of a promise or a treaty. Those most robbed and outraged by this bandit give him credit for complying strictly to his word. Like a rattlesnake, he generally warned before he struck. Two things he has never done — he has never committed arson, nor offered to insult white females. In these two things may be traced his cavalier blood."

Giles Leach struggled with the situation, as did Mary Norment. Here are excerpts from his sworn and examined statements in Washington:

Q. What are these people; are they negroes?

A. Well sir, I desire to tell you the truth as near as I can; but I do not know they are; I think they are a mixture of Spanish, Portuguese, and Indian. About half of them have straight black hair, and many of the characteristics of the Cherokee Indians in our state; then, as they amalgamate and mix, the hair becomes curly and kinky, and from that down to real woolen hair.

Q. You think they are mixed negroes and Indians?

A. I think they are mixed Portuguese, Spaniards, and Indians; I mean to class the Spaniards and Portuguese as one class, and the Indians as another. I do not think that in that class of the population there is much negro blood at all; about half of the colored population that I have attemped to describe all have always been free; I was born among them and I recken I know them perfectly well. They are a thriftless, lazy, thievish and indolent population. They are called "mulattoes;" that is the name they are known by, as contradistinguished from negroes.

Later questions by the Chairman, Mr. Poole:

Q. I understand you to say that these seven or eight hundred persons that you designate as mulattoes are not negroes, but are a mixture of Portuguese and Spanish, white blood and Indian blood; you think they are not generally negroes?

A. I do not think that the negro blood predominates.

Q. The word "mulatto" means a cross between a white and negro?

All the different characters in this drama had an agenda. The chairman tried to direct his questioing toward an Indian derivative to justify their punishment. Mary Norment leaned toward these people being mulatto or black. She began with them being "shufflers," as blacks always shuffled; this their home town, Scuffletown. She contradicted herself in concluding that they raided by painting their faces black, as they were disguising their savage Indian features. "So endures the culture of domination, while the world it was rooted in crumbles and is rebuilt with both the opposition and labors of its victims."

Who did the Lowerys say they were? Sometimes they were Indians, and sometimes they said they were "Melungeons." Indian removal to the West and disfranchisement of free persons of color happened in a context where one's racial identity determined one's own destiny.[16]

A much later revival of the Lumbee theory was revisited by Hamilton McMillan. When the Lumbee Indians claimed a heritage to Roanoke, McMillin was intriguted with the idea and the problems with the legalities of living as darker-skinned persons (mulattos) in the late 1800s. They had declined to go to all-black schools and were largely uneducated and clannish. He thought he detected some of them having the same early Anglo-Saxon language and names as those of the people of 1587. He took the case all the way to the General Assembly, and laws were passed calling the people Croatoan Indians and providing them with their own schools and teachers. In spite of recognition, the Indians continued to have economic problems and petitioned the federal government for official recognition of their tribal status. In 1915, Special Agent O.M. McPherson wrote, "I have no hesitancy in expressing the belief that the Indians who originally settled in Robeson and adjoining counties in North Carolina were an amalgamation of the Hatteras Indians with Gov. White's lost colony."[17]

Later historians disputed the Lumbees as the Lost Colonists. They felt the unique Anglo-Saxon speech was only a dialect found in several other places along the coast. Names that McMillin had thought to be carried from the colonists to the Lumbee were not unique to this particular group. They also found that legislation passed in favor of the Lumbees passed under pressure from McMillan and the Indians themselves. Thus disappeared another theory of Lost Colonists and perhaps later, Melungeons. The entire study is another example of a people absorbed as inconsequental in the settlement of America by Anglo-Saxons.

Archaeological excavations continue today in areas surrounding Roanoke Island, and perhaps someday objects will be found in the area to tie the Lost Colonists to some former culture. David Phelps, head of the East Carolina coastal office of Archaeology, reported finding a 16th century gold signet ring in what is believed to be the Croatan Indian culture on Hatteras Island. The ring seemed to be the type used to sign and seal documents. The early colonists were about 45 miles north of this area.[18]

We must remember in this discussion that further archaeological digs may complicate rather than simplify this area and its potential, as the 116 men, women, and children left by White in 1587 were not the only European settlers abandoned in the New World prior to Jamestown. Lane left at least three people when he departed with Drake. Grenville left at least 15 when he departed. The area was populated with Spanish even prior to the tragedies of the English colonists. Spanish friers tried to establish an outpost on the Chesapeake before this period and the French Charlesfort was in existence in 1562. As we recall, the Indians had told of shipwrecks twenty years prior to Amadas and Barlowe. We know Drake was certainly suspect in abandoning captured slaves wherever he could recklessly perceive the chance for excitement or profit. Many of these early theories considered only abandoned or lost males, but the physically dominant aggressors of the species would find a way to perpetuate the race in any alien environment.

By now, we can begin to see how complicated it has become to try to identify the origin of darker-skinned people living amoung predominatley lighter-skinned Anglo-Saxons. The Phoenicians, Welsh, Berbers/Moors, or even the Lost Colonists are possible ancestors of these people. We will continue the quest of their history in the next chapter.

---

[1]David Stick, *From Roanoke Island, The Beginning of English America.* University of North Carolina Press 1983, pp. 27-35.

[2]ibid

[3]John R. Swanton, *The Indian Tribes of North America,* Smithsonian Institution Press, Washinton D. C., 1969, pp. 81-83

[4]David Stick, ibid.

[5]Ivor Noel Hume, *The Virginia Adventure,* University Press of Virginia, Charlottesville, 1994, p. 55.

[6]David Beers Quinn, *The Lost Colonists,* North Carolina Department of Cultural Resources, Raleigh, North Carolina, 1984.

[7]Ibid

[8]David Stick, ibid

[9]Ivor Noel Hume, ibid

[10]David Beers Quinn, ibid

[11]Joseph Judge, "Exploring Our Forgotten Century," National Geographic, Washington D. C., Volume 173, Number 3, March 1988.

[12]David Beers Quinn, ibid

[13]ibid

[14]David Stick, ibid

[15]David Beers Quinn, ibid

[16]Gerald M. Sider, *Lumbee Indian Histories*, Cambridge University Press, 1993, New York, New York, pp. 162-163

[17]David Stick, ibid

[18]Arlee Gowen, Gowen Research Foundation, Lubbock, Texas,Volume 10, Number 2 October 1988

Chapter 9
Onward To Newman's Ridge

We will deal in this chapter with the period after the 1700s, when there may have been Melungeons leaving the Eastern regions and fleeing to the frontiers. Perhaps some isolated people besides the Native Americans were already scattered in the interior over the mountains much before this time, but a reliable confirmation is hard to find. There was a reasonable concentration of non-Native Americans, or Melungeons, in the East Tennessee area by 1790.

The following were exerpts from persons speaking of other people in the interior. As we discussed earlier, in the letters of Abraham Wood, of 1673, a reference was made to: "Eight dayes jorney down this river lives a white people which have long beardes and whiskers and weares clothing, and on some of ye other rivers lives a hairey people."[1] Some scholors interpreted this historical statement as meaning people other than Indians were living somewhere in the proximity of the present state of Tennessee. Williams footnoted the above encounter with the possibility of the whites

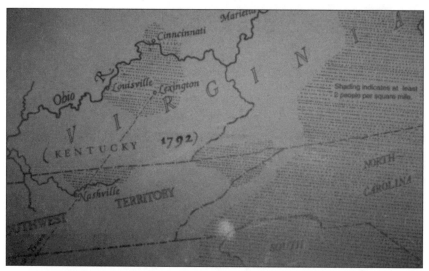

Concentrations in the Interior. Courtesy of Falls of the Ohio Museum.

observed by Abraham Wood being Spaniards, because they had been in contact with Cherokees in the gold area of the southern Alleghanies as early as 1654.

The Wood letter told of 20 Tomahittans (Yuchi) going to the white people's village with furs to trade. He says, "They (the whites) killed tenn of them and put ye other tenn in irons." He went on to say that they had many blacks as well as many swine and cattle, and they had a brick building. Wood also spoke of the Yuchi Indians as having, "gunnes, not such locks as oures bee, the steeles are long and channelld where ye flints strike." The Yuchi had many brass, "potts and kettles from three gallons to thirty. They have two mullato women; all ye white and black people they take they put to death."[2] Some scholars interpreted this entire report to mean that Melungeons were the described whites, and that they lived in the East Tennessee area prior to and in 1673.

The Cherokees had migrated from somewhere in the Northeast in very early times. Eventually, they migrated south and occupied Tennessee and North Carolina, parts of South Carolina, Georgia, Alabama, and Virginia. This vast territory comprised 40,000 square miles. They were a large tribe of 22,000 in 1600 and were held in check from further expansion in the Southeast by the Powhatan with 6,000 members and the Monacan with 1,200.[3]

The persistant myths of the Cherokee told of their arrival in their Southeastern home to find white settlers already participating in agricuture and other permanent activites in the area. This migration date was oral and vague, but varies from genesis to 1200-1400 A.D.

In 1797, an investigator by the name of Barton said, "Reports by the Cheerake tell us, that when they first arrived in the country which they inhabit, they found it possessed by certain 'moon-eyed people', who could not see in the day time. These wretches they expelled." He seems to consider them an albino race.[4]

In 1823, Haywood told of the Cherokee finding "white people" near the head of the Little Tennessee River with forts all the way to Chickamauga Creek. Other tribes spoke of the white people also being in Kentucky and extending across a part of Tennessee. He described them as living in circular houses made of upright logs, and covered with earth excavated from deep inside.[5]

A "halfbreed" by the name of Harry Smith told of a tradition of a small pure-white people who lived on the site of a large mound on the northern side of the Hiawassee near present-day Murphy, North Carolina.

In 1750, Dr. Thomas Walker went on one of his many wilderness explorations to the area of Sneedville, Tennessee, where he found what he called the "Carmel Indians."[6]

By 1775, John Sevier, another prominent pioneer of the time, addressed a similiar story by letter to the governor of North Carolina. Sevier knew the area well, as he had been dispatched by Governor Dumore of Virginia to rid the west of the Indian problem in Lord Dunmore's War. Just five years prior to the war, a few settlers reported finding the Melungeons, who were said to have been there for 200 years. Sevier personally crossed the mountains in 1775 and found some of these same people, described earlier as Melungeons, near Harrogate, Tennessee. He wrote of the dark-skinned people having, "straight black hair and dark blue eyes."[7]

The mound stories are a series of theories covering many possible people, but will only be mentioned here in the context of the Melungeons. As early as 1781, Thomas Jefferson had been fascinated with the huge earthern structures observed near Monticello. He conducted digs of the mounds for artifacts to add to his collections. (As noted earlier, most of his excellent documented artifacts were sold and disappeared after his death.) The people of his time, whites and Indians alike, were fascinated but puzzled over the builders of these huge, magnificent engineering feats.

Jefferson could not attribute the engineering to Native Americans for his prejudices rendered them incapable. Jefferson felt the mounds were the product of a superior white civilization. Perhaps he was correct in believing that these people might have been only the survivors of an earlier, more progressive, race. After all, civilization is not always upward from the savage to our great technological age. Disease, wars, changes of priorities, and lack of funds contribute to some steps forward and a few backward throughout time.

Unfortunately, there are no available answers to a possible Melungeon connection with these early discoveries, as eventual westward migrations and land clearing destoyed most of these majectic earthen structures.[8] The encroaching migrants had little interest in analyzing the mounds.

Early testimonials are examples of the multitude of theories that became facts of the Melungeons settling on the frontier, prior to any other non-Indians. It is likely some sparsely populated pockets of people may have survived from the many early people lost, deserted, or abandoned as they struggled on the new frontier. Theoretically, these small groups (if they were outcasts due to skin color) were known of in the East and became a beacon for those trying to migrate westward to avoid discrimination for color. It seems reasonable to believe the Tri-state Triangle started with some non-whites and developed the reputation as a refuge for darker outcasts. The general area was the location of dark peoples who had migrated from diverse sections of the country.

We studied a few of the earlier discrimination cases against the Lumbee. These types of violations happened in the Tri-state Triangle, and they have happened throughout the world, as one group strived for domination and material gain over another. The French, Spanish, Portuguese, Indians, Negroes, and others became fair game for the British, as they rose to power with whomever they chose as their fair-skinned allies. The Melungeons were only a small obstacle in their quest for control of the continent and its resources.

Those that were in control also mandated laws in their realization that legal order was necessary for civilization in the midst of chaos. The formation and the interpretion of laws are the privilege of those in control. In the early years, laws affecting voting, taxes, and the ability to defend oneself varied from state to state. Unfavorable state laws were passed over the years which caused the Melungeons to flee westward away from the population pressures. These circumstances eventually caused them to be as reclusive as possible.

For example, even today such people wanting to blend into the surroundings can be very elusive. An ex-census worker from Morristown, Tennessee, who was exhibiting at the Mountain Makins Art Show was interviewed. He had been employed by the federal government to survey the population of Hancock County. His data sheet of a previous census listed a rather large family by the name of Gibson up a remote road. He could not find the target family, and nobody knew of their residence. The census taker had surveyed and listed everybody on the road except this one family. He stopped at a small store at the end of the road and began to subtly interrogate the local customers. One man seemed to know a considerable amount about the Gibsons, but he didn't know where they lived. He confirmed they still lived somewhere in the area. He knew all the names of the children but few details of their ages. He didn't know the head of the household's place of employment, but he knew much of his work habits. He knew many of the idiosyncrasies of the wife, but he didn't know if she worked or her age. The skills of the census worker finally allowed him to risk the question, "Just what is your name?" The man could have been evasive, but his answer was, "Gibson!"

There were variations in dates and substance from state to state, but the intent and provisions were all basically similar: Whites were protected against any contested violation of any properties; laws were for white control, subservience, and subordination of designated minorities, who had no standing in the courts, no right to vote, no right to make contracts, and could not strike a white man in self-defense, and the killing of a minority was seldom regarded as murder.[9]

The classification applied frequently to the Melungeons was part Negro/mulatto/free colored. An example of laws that were enacted is in 1775, a North Carolina free colored could be taxed. "In 1794, Tennessee declared all Negroes, Indians, Mulattos, and all persons of mixed blood, descended from Negro or Indian ancestors to the third generation inclusive, whether bond or free, to be incapable in law to be witness in any case whatsoever, except against each other, no person, thus qualified, can be a witness, in a State prosecution, for a defendant who belongs to one of the disqualified classes."[10] In 1796, Tennessee amended this law to allow every freeman of the age of twenty-one and above to vote.

States also passed laws at different times concerning who might be classified as tithable persons to be taxed. Reclassified people sometimes fled to other states to avoid new laws of taxation.

In 1820, people were enumerated in the census in four categories: (1) whites, (2) slaves, (3) free persons of color, and (4) all other persons except Indians not taxed (Indians not taxed were not enumerated). The forth class seems to be designed for Indians living as

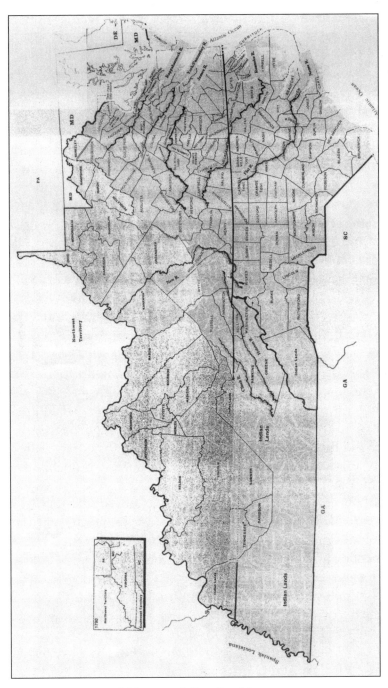

Melungeon Migration Map.
Courtesy of William Thorndale & William Dollarhide

ordinary citizens, if Indians who were not taxed were considered as "other persons." Free persons of color implied Negro blood.[11]

In 1834, Tennessee significantly changed the meaning of their earlier law by allowing only free white men twenty-one and older the right to vote. This session also exempted men of color from military duty in time of peace, and also from paying a free poll tax. J. W. Caldwell says that prior to 1834 free Negroes were allowed to vote in Tennessee, and the privilege had caused a mass influx of people of the category from North Carolina and other states. The new law was passed by Tennessee as a protective measure.[12]

We can attempt to trace a general migratory route (page 137) for some of the Melungeons who eventually settled in Western Virginia and Eastern Tennessee. Eventually, these people stopped their migration in East Tennessee where many other dark people were already established prior to the Tennessee voting law of 1834. This map illustrates potential population movements from the east and south with considerations only for North Carolina and Virginia. The Flat River and the New River in Orange County, North Carolina were inward points from the coast of South Carolina. Notice the close proximity of any Melungeon movements to those rivers and the many other rivers and streams, which were the pioneer highways. The Nottoway, James, Roanoke, Rapidan, Faquire, Rappahannock, Pamunkey, Appomattox, Dan, Kanahwa, Clinch, Holston, and Blackwater (which could have significance as to the name of the Blackwater Creek in Vardy Valley) were probably used by various people heading westward.

In Virginia, the migrating dark people moved eastward from the coast and were found in Albemarle, Louisa, and Hanover Counties. Eventually, many moved westward to Bedford County and onward to the long and winding New River. Some were issued land grants on the New River (for example Vardy Collins) and remained there for a period during westward migration. For those desiring racial equality, primitive communications of the day slowly carried words of encouragement to migrate further west to the "melting pot" of this equality at the concurrence of the three states of Tennessee, Virginia, and North Carolina.

The eastern Tennessee people that can be traced began to settle into their final home by the late 1700s to early 1800s. Some passed

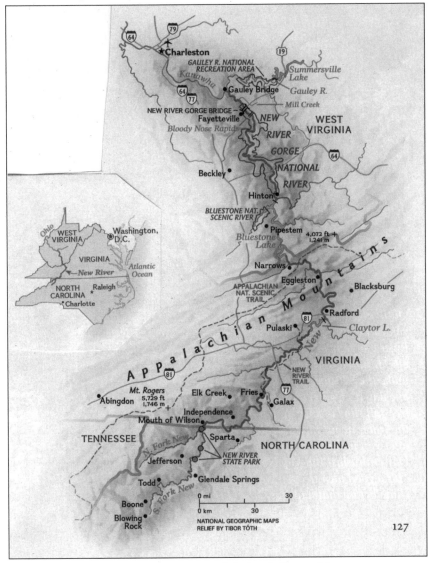

New River. Courtesy of National Geographic.

through Fort Blackmore and attended the Stoney Creek Baptist Church before entering Blackwater, Vardy, Sneedville, and Newman's Ridge. The three state triangle of Western Virginia, Western North Carolina, and Eastern Tennessee proved to be an opportune area for movement to avoid various activities involved with discriminatory laws or harassment from lighter-skinned neighbors.

Detail New River. Courtesy of National Geographic.

The mountainous terrain also contributed to their desire for isolation. In their future, the frontier would close in around them, and eventually, they would lose knowledge and even motivation to seek opportunities beyond their newly chosen haven of isolation.

The initial isolation and limited gene pool were not factors that proved too detrimental, as hardy children were born in great numbers. Much, much later we heard of them having such Mediterranean diseases such as thalassemia, familial Mediterranean fever, and sarcoidosis. Today, some symptoms are diagnosed as lupus. Before our knowledge of these uniquely Mediterranean diseases, these people seemed to have no more problem living on the frontier than the ordinary pioneer. Adult onset diabetes and goiter problems seemed to be diagnosable and fairly common, but it did not deter them from living a full life with normal productivity.

The information in this Appendix was taken from the 1830 census records of Hawkins and Grainger Counties in Tennessee. The (fc) means "free persons of color."

Hawkins County, Tennessee - 1830
(Heads of Families)

Fountain Goen (fc)	Harden Goen (fc)
George Goen (fc)	Samuel Mullens (fc)
John Goen (fc)	William Nichols (fc)
Betsy Goen (fc)	John Minor (fc)
Zachariah Minor (fc)	Thomas Hale (fc)
Wiatt Collins (fc)	Millenton Collins (fc)
Andrew Collins (fc)	James Collins (fc)
Martin Collins (fc)	Charles Gibson (fc)
John Collins (fc)	Esau Gibson (fc)
Martin Collins (fc)	Cherod Gibson (fc)
Simeon Collins (fc)	Joseph F. Gibson (fc)
Vardy Collins (fc)	Andrew Gibson (fc)
Mary Collins (fc)	Sheppard Gibson (fc)
Levi Collins (fc)	Jordon Gibson (fc)
Benjamin Collins (fc)	Polly Gibson (fc)
Edmund Collins (fc)	Jonathan Gibson (fc)
Betsy Jones (fc)	Jesse Gibson (fc)
Edmund Goodman (fc)	Jordan Goodman (fc)
James Moore (fc)	Burton Cold (fc)
Dicey Bowling (fc)	Michael Bowling (fc)
Charles Beare (fc)	Henry Mosely (fc)
Timothy Williams (fc)	

Grainger County, Tennessee - 1830
(Heads of Families)

Edmund Bolen (fc)	Ezekiel Bolen (fc)
Shadrach Bolen (fc)	Clabourn Bolen (fc)
Edmund Bolen (fc)	Moses Collins (fc)

Melungeon Names. Courtesy of Bonnie Ball.

The continued isolation and reclusive habits of the Melungeons resulted in a few key names being associated with them. If people had the names listed on page 141, lived in the tri-state area, and had dark features, they would most likely be a Melungeon. Note "f.c." after a name designated free colored. Some names, found in the census with Portuguese given to identify nationality, were marked through and replaced by "free colored."

Dr. Virginia DeMarce studied Melungeon names and found Collins to be the most frequent. Some other common names that she encountered were: Bell, Moore, Brogan, Bunch, Denham, Williams, and Sexton. Dr. DeMarce also listed some whites who later inter-married with Melungeons such as the Lawsons and Delps.[13] The Delps eventually became darker than those in the immediate area. Mother referred to them as, "Them ole black Deps."

Variations of spelling confuse some of the early names, such as

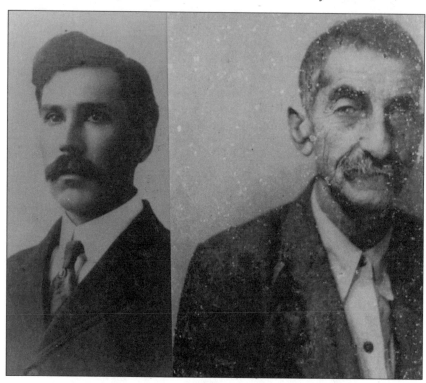

People with Collins Name
Left- LeHam Collins-Courtesy of Ruth Muhlbauer
Right- Bud Rand Collins-Courtesy of Henry Swiney (deceased) Pete Swiney.

the family name Goen. This particular name has been found to have over thirty different spellings (Gwinn to Goings). Bowling also has multiple spellings (Bolen to Bolton). Other Melungeon names in the Hancock County, Tennessee, area were Sizemore, Miser, Green, Jones, Davidson, Seal, Seals, Lovin, Hatfield, Bunch, Hopkins, and Rhea, with Swineys, Hortons, and Stewarts frequently intermarrying with the Melungeons.

A Collins, a Goins, and a Davidson
Courtesy of W.C. Collins
Left to right Hagan Collins, Simeon Goins, and Hobart Davidson

---

[1]Samuel Cole Williams, *Early Travels in the Tennessee Country 1540-1800*, The Watauga Press, Johnson City, Tennessee, 1928, pp. 28-29.
[2]ibid
[3]John R. Swanton, *The Indian Tribes of North America*, Smithsonian Institution Press, New York, New York, 1952.
[4]James Mooney, *Myths of the Cherokee and Sacred Formulas of the Cherokees*, Cherokee Heritage Books, Elders' Bookstore, Charles and Randy Elder, Nashville, Tennessee, 1982, pp. 21-22.

[5]ibid

[6]James Morgan, "The Melungeon," National Observer, April 9, 1977.

[7]*The Family Tree,* The Odom Library, Moultrie, Georgia, Oct/Nov, 1993.

[8]Mooney, ibid 21-22

[9]*Colliers Encyclopedia,* P.F. Collier and Son Corporation, New York, 1955, Volume 14, p. 461.

[10]Meigs Tennessee Supreme Court Reports, Volume 1, 1882 p. 19.

[11]Sandra Keyes Ivey, *Oral, Printed, and Popular Culture Traditions Related To The Melungeons of Hancock County,Tennessee,* University Microfilms International, Ann Arbor, Michigan, Indiana University, Ph.D. 1976, p. 182.

[12]J. W. Caldwell, *Studies in the Constitutional History of Tennessee,* 2nd Edition, Cincinnati: 1907, p. 148.

[13]Virginia Easley DeMarce, *Melungeons, Family Name by Family Name,* National Genealogical Society presentation, Arlington, Virginia, May 1996.

Chapter 10
Early Settlers and Their Culture

Micager Bunch, Benjamin Collins, Solomon Collins, Valentine Collins, Vardemon Collins, Wyatt Collins, Shepard Gibson, Joseph Goings, Jim Mullins, and others were some of the known migrators to the Lee County, Virginia and Hawkins County, Newman's Ridge, Tennessee area in the late 1700s to early 1800s. Many of the Collins people were thought to be related. (Three of the above list are three times great- and four times great-grandfathers of the author.)

What nationality were these people, and what type of culture did they have? Let's examine some of the lives, theories, and myths of this small representation of the core group of Newman's Ridge. Unfortunately, we have very little visual representations of this group, but we do have some old tintypes in various conditions of preservation of a few early scenes and later descendants. Below is a picture of early life on Newman's Ridge. The photo on page 146 is of Vardy Valley at the base of Newman's Ridge and the Powell Mountains. Mulberry Gap Road splits the valley into north and south. Vardy Valley, with Blackwater Creek in the center, is one-quarter to one-half mile wide and runs east. To the west, the valley is called Snake Hollow.

In 1891, William Allen Dromgoole (a writer who was mentioned in earlier chapters) lived on Newman's Ridge with a family for a lengthy period to study the people and their lineage. Current historians question many of her conclusions, but she did not appear to be totally in error. After all, this was near the end of the decline

Newman's Ridge.
Courtesy of John Mullins III (deceased)
Aileen Mullins

Vardy Valley. Courtesy of Ellen Trent (deceased) David Trent.

of Melungeons as free people, and they were now surrounded in their own small refuge. They were no longer on the frontier. Her writings introduce us to some of the above people in her study, "The Malungeon Tree And Its Four Branches."

Dromgoole started her analysis in the late 1700s with the statement that Vardy Collins was the source of the origional inhabitants. She felt that all the Collinses were Indians, with names acquired from white men while living in Virginia, before migrating to North Carolina and eventually to Tennessee. The original group, and others who followed, were all called "the Collins tribe."

She stated that people descended from a particular person were named individual given names and their surnames were those of the father or mother of their tribe (for example Benjamin Collins' offspring would be Andrew Ben, Zeke Ben, etc.) to differentiate between the many Collinses. For example, if Jordon Ben (son of Benjamin Collins) were to marry Abby Sol (daughter of Solomon Collins), they would have a son called Callaway Abbey after his mother. Before marriage, the daughter took her father's given name; after marriage, she took that of her husband. For example, Calloway's wife was Ann Calloway. Over time, the Collinses prospered, and their increased numbers necessitated the formation of clans, which retained the names of key leaders (Ben clan, Sol clan).

Dromgoole reported these first Indian Collinses lived in single rooms on beds of leaves, with only the necessities for clothing. She described them as smoking and dreaming away the days in the delightful environs of Newman's Ridge.

Her article has an Englishman-Irishman trapper by the name of Jim Mullins entering the isolated community to introduce the first white blood, as well as the beginning of the second largest tribe to the Collinses. Dromgoole also wrote that the Mullins tribe was the strongest, as well as the most daring and obstinate. She described Jim Mullins as roving, daring, and having the free disposition of the Indians. He was said to be a great participant in sports and was always "cheek by jowl" with the Cherokees and other Indian tribes on the frontier. She reinterated that he married a relative of old Sol Collins and reared a family known as the Mullins tribe.

Dromgoole introduced an African branch to the Melungeons with a Goins migrating from North Carolina at the time of Tennessee statehood. She had him settling nearby in Powell's Valley instead of on Newman's Ridge. Goins "took up" with a Melungeon woman and formed the Goins tribe. This group had kinky hair, flat noses and feet, thick lips, and a complexion unlike the Collins and Mullins tribe. The Goinses, claim they were Portuguese. This group was always looked upon by the other Melungeons with contempt, and they were rejected socially and politically, although some shiftless stragglers from other tribes were to have intermarried with the Goinses.

Dromgoole described the forth branch of the Melungeons as being slow to decipher, but finally she traced them to a Portuguese by the name of Denham, who married a Collins. (David Denham, a mulatto, did marry Solomon Collins' sister, Elizabeth. They lived in the Mulberry area.) She stated every runaway or straggler passing through the country eventually "took up" with the Melungeons (then called Ridgemanites). She characterized them as harmless, social, and good-natured when comfortable with a person, but, at first, suspicious, distant, and morose.

According to some theories, Denham migrated from one of the southern Spanish colonies to Mulberry Creek. Denham was said to have followed his instincts to the mountains of what was then the North Carolina territory and then onward to Newman's Ridge.

Another theory had him descended from slaves from Jamaica. In 1655, England did wrest Jamaica from Spain, and 1500 Spanish slaves fled to the mountains to multiply and become known as "mountain negroes" or "maroons." These "maroons" were frequently used as shipmates by the Portuguese, who were known to the competition as the most daring and terrible on the seas. As would be expected, frequent insubordination resulted in castoffs on shore.

Dromgoole rejected the (unfortunate) mixture to the Portuguese branch of the Melungeons by the Negro Goins, who repudiated his African streak under the guise of being Portuguese. She did say the Negro and Portuguese branches are obviously different, as skin tones are easily discernable.

She suggested, in 1891, that Melungeons were slow to progress. They were still living in huts, with Indian characteristics and customs, and they remained exclusive and seclusive as sons of the forest.[1]

What do we learn from this discriminitory study of the Melungeons in 1891? The named people in her discussion did exist, but they were not necessarily of the nationality she described. As Dromgoole reiterates, these people were noticably darker in varying degrees or looked different than the white Anglo-Saxons who later entered their isolated territory. In appearance, many did not fit the absolute, but always subjective, category of Negro or Indian. The various census reports were likewise inconsistent in labeling them as white or free colored. There were also frequent attempts to send them to Negro schools, which they rejected, but occasionally, they were known to slip into areas of Negro communities for other physical interactions.

She said they lived similiar to the Indians in the area, but, perhaps, because of the lack of equal opportunities, anybody would have lived in the same manner. Their so-called dreamy lifestyle spent smoking tobacco in the seclusion of Newman's Ridge would probably have been all that was available for entertainment, after enough food had been grown or gathered for survival. Her Portuguese theory was probably a natural development, since older Melungeons have always called themselves, "Portugee." There must have been some basis for this term, because it is heard within the populace to this day. Certainly it would have been advantageous for dark minorities to be labled Portuguese over the rival Spanish. If language were not a factor, it would have been difficult to differentiate Portuguese characteristics or heritage from those of the Spanish.

Of the Dromgoole Melungeon characters, Vardy Collins is probably the best known. Some things we know about him are fact, but most are conjecture. He was born in 1764 in Grayson County, Virginia (census reported North Carolina), near the North Carolina line on the New River. The town was called Mouth of Wilson. Some say Vardy was a full-blooded Indian. Martha Collins, deceased, who is pictured in chapter seven, is a direct decendant. Martha said Vardy, or Vardimen's, name was Navarre (Melungeon spelling Navarrh) which is Portuguese or Spanish.

Vardy married Peggy Gibson, born 1771-1773, who was said to be Spanish and sometimes called "Spanish" Peggy. Their descendants were described as dark with straight, black hair. A few, though, had a wave in the hair, some even had kinky hair. This trait was thought to have come from the Spanish or the Irish mixture of the Mullins, or later marriages with the Scots-Irish. The household was listed as free colored in the 1830 census of Tennessee.

Vardy was listed in Wilkes County, North Carolina, in 1795 and Ashe County in 1800. Ashe was formed from Wilkes in 1810, and Grayson County, Virginia, was just above on the Virginia line; therefore, he may have lived in the general area prior to migrating to East Tennessee in 1809. He received land grants in North Carolina in 1790 and 1793.

Vardy owned the Vardy Valley area from the Lee County, Virginia line to Mulberry Gap. (See the Vardy Valley photo on page 146). Vardy and Peggy moved to a big house near Vardy (Sulphur) Springs and raised a family of eight. They had similiar activities to any other free persons of the era. They had at least eight Tennessee land grants, testified in court, and he served as executor in deaths of several local residents.

Vardy Sulphur Springs
Courtesy of Hughie and Laura Mullins (deceased)
Carl & Betty Mullins Hilton, R.C. & Marcie Mullins

The interesting stories about the source of his wealth are unsubstantiated. Some thought Peggy, his wife, had been wealthy. Others thought he had been a pirate and met Peggy while serving on the Spanish Main. His home did serve as hostel and lodging for weary travelers, as well as health enthusiasts for the nearby Vardy Sulphur Springs. Rumors are that few people with wealth ever left his home alive. William Grohse surmised a better thought: Perhaps he came by his money honestly and practiced the open and free hospitality of the back woods. He continued that "likely he was a man of force and resolute habit, and likely envied by the less successful, and suspected where there was but little truth or little cause for it."[2]

Dromgoole told another story, specifically of Vardy and his brother-in-law Shepard "Buck" Gibson, going for wealth in a different manner. She began with the two using the cunning of their Cherokee ancestors to set up a scheme for themselves in the almost unbroken Territory of North Carolina. Old Buck (Shepard) added additional color to Vardy's skin and went to Richmond, Virginia, with Vardy posed as his slave. Vardy found unsuspecting parties interested in the fine physical prospect of his brother-in-law and traded Shepard his "likely nigger" for a wagon, mules, a lot of other goods, and three hundred dollars in cash. Once outside Richmond, the two headed toward the wilderness of North Carolina as previously planned. They removed the disguise, divided their loot, and pursued a new life westward toward Newman's Ridge. Droomgoole swore the story was truly from Vardy and his descendants, as she stated Vardy lived to a ripe old age and repeated the story many times. She added that the Gibson and Collins names were also stolen from white settlers from Virginia.[3] This story has been repeated in many places throughout the lore of the Melungeons. If only partially true, it shows definite dark coloration and good physical characteristics in these particular individuals with a mental awareness and cunning to deal with the strata of the population involved in slavery.

Below is a descendant of Shepard Gibson, the Reverend Delmont "Seven" Gibson of Elm Springs Babtist Church in Snake Hollow.

Vardy's descendants, by family tradition, managed a boarding house after his death. The picture below shows Vardy's grandchildren, Batie and Cynthia Collins in center, with their four children. Batie was the son of Alfred (Vardy's son) and Cynthia was actually the daughter of George Goins and Frankie Bunch (Frankie's first husband was Simeon, Vardy's son). George Goins was son of Joseph Goins.

Descendant of Shep Gibson
Photography by
Ann Callahan
Courtesy of
Delmont Gibson

Vardy Boarding House
Courtesy of Ellen Trent
(deceased)
David Trent

This amusing but discriminitory letter of 1849 follows our quest for the real Vardy. It began, "You must know that within some ten miles of this owl's nest, there is a watering-place, known hereabouts as 'Blackwater Springs.' It is situated in a narrow gorge, scarcely half a mile wide, between Powell's Mountain and Newman's Ridge, and is, as you may suppose, almost inaccessible. A hundred men could defend the pass against even an Xerxian army. Now this gorge and the tops and sides of the adjoining mountains are inhabited by a singular species of the human animal called Melungeons."

The letter continued as a stop was made at "Old Vardy's, the hostelrie of the vicinage. Old Vardy was the 'Chief cook and bottle-washer' of the Melungeons, and was really a very clever fellow, but his hotel savored strongly of that peculiar perfume that one may find in the sleeping rooms of our negro servants, especially on a close, warm, summer's evening. We arrived at Vardy's in time for supper, and, that despatched, we went to the spring, where were assembled several rude log huts, and a small sprinkling of 'the natives,' together with a fiddle and other preparations for a dance. Shoes, stockings, and coats were unknown luxuries among them — at least, we saw them not.

"The dance was engaged in with right hearty good will, and would have put to the blush the tame steppings of our beaux. Among the participants was a tall, raw-boned damsel, with her two garmets fluttering readily in the amorous night breeze, whose black eyes were lit up with an unusual fire, either from repeated visits to the nearest hut, behind the door of which was placed an open-mouthed stone jar of new-made corn whiskey, and in which was a gourd, with a 'deuce a bit' of sugar at all, and no water nearer than the spring. Nearest her on the right was a lank, lantern-jawed, high-cheeked, long-legged fellow, who seemed similarly elevated. Now these two, Jord Bilson, (that was he), and Syl Varmin, (that was she), were destined to afford the amusement of the evening; for Jord, in cutting the pidgeon-wing, chanced to light from one of his aerial flights right upon the ponderous petal appendage of Syl, a compliment which this amiable lady seemed in no way disposed to accept kindly.

"'Jord Bilson,' said the tender Syl, 'I'll thank you to keep your darned hoofs off my feet.'

"'Oh, Jord's feet are so tarnel big he can't manage 'em all by his-self,' suggested some pacificator nearby.

"'He'll have to keep 'em off me,'suggested Syl, 'or I'll shorten 'em for him.'

"'Now look ye here, Syl Varmin,' answered Jord, somewhat net-tled at both remarks, 'I didn't go to tread on your feet, but I don't want you to be cutting up any rusties about. You're nothing but a crossgrained critter, anyhow.'

"'And you're a darned Melungeon.'

"'Well, if I am, I aint nigger-Melungeon, anyhow — I'm Indian-Melungeon, and that's more an you is.'

"'See here, Jord,' said Syl, now highly nettled, 'I'll give you a dol-lor ef you'll go out on the grass and fight it out.'

"Jord smiled faintly and demurred, adding — 'Go home, Syl, and look under you puncheons and see ef you can't fill a bed outen the hair of them hogs you stole from Vardy.'

"'And you go to the Sow's cave, Jord Bilson, ef it comes to that, and see how many shucks you got offen that corn you tuck from Pete Jomen. Will you take the dollar?'

"Jord now seemed about to consent, and Syl reduced the pre-mium by one half, and finally came down to a quarter, and then Jord began to offer a quarter, a half, and finally a dollar; but Syl's prudence equalled his, and seeing that neither was likely to accept, we returned to our hotel, and were informed by old Vardy that the sight we had witnessed was no 'onusual one. The boys and girls was jist having a little fun.'

"And so it proved, for about midnight we were awakened by a loud noise of contending parties in fierce combat, and, rising and looking out from the chinks of our hut, we saw the whole party engaged in a grand melee; rising above the din of all which, was the harsh voice of Syl Varmin, calling out —

"'Stand back here Sal Frazer, and let me do the rest of the beaten of Jord Bilson; I haint forgot his roofs yit.'

"The melee closed, and we retired again, and by breakfast next morning all hands were reconciled, and the stone jar was replen-ished out of the mutual pocket, and peace and quiet ruled where so lately all had been recriminitions and blows.

— 153 —

Howard Collins & Daughter. Courtesy of Ellen Trent (deceased)
David Trent

"After breakfast, just as the supper had been at old Jack's save only that here we had a table, we started for the Clinch River for a day's fishing, where other and yet more amusing incidents awaited us. But as I have dwelt upon this early part of the journey longer than I intended, you must wait till the next letter for the concluding incidents."[4]

Thus closed the story of discrimination, which included even different classes of Melungeon with inferences of part-Negro bloodlines being less equal than part-Indian.

Another descendant of Vardy that was well known in the area was grandson Howard Collins, born of Simeon and Frankie Bunch Collins. Simeon was son of Vardy, as mentioned previously.

"Big" Howard Collins was so nicknamed because he was over six feet tall and weighed over 200 pounds. The photo also shows his children to be large, as Docia, the daughter in the picture who weighed at least 250 pounds. His personality was described as forceful, strong, and obstinate, but with a skill to influence others. He served as a private in Company E, 2nd Tennessee Cavalry from 1861-1864 and suffered from chronic diahrrea as a result of his tour of duty.

He was considered fairly well-to-do financially. "Big" Howard

Howard Collins' Home. Courtesy of Ellen Trent (deceased) David Trent.

owned a grist mill on Blackwater Creek, as well as farmland and practiced the usual "moonshine" activites of the area. At one time, two persons were found hanged in his mill, and he was charged with murder. Eventually, he was pardoned for the offense. Pictures of his home appear to confirm his prosperity (page 155).

Another key Melungeon of the early settlers in the Newman's Ridge area of East Tennessee was Joseph Goings Jr. The man and his family were an example of the elusiveness of the data confirming some type of pattern of these mystery people and their life styles. The author has pursued this man and his kin for thirty years, from Bedford County, Virginia to Hawkins and Hancock County, Tennessee, with little confirmed evidence to present over previous rumors and myths.

He was thought to have been born in 1766-73, somewhere in Eastern Virginia, perhaps Bedford or Albemarle County according to deceased Vardy historian, William Grohse. Census records confuse the attempt to confirm which of the various Joseph Goings is the one who ended up in East Tennessee. The name Goings has been spelled over thirty different ways over the years, but upon examination of all possible spellings, the family lineage remains elusive.

Vardy historian William Grohse reported Joseph Goings Sr. served in the Revolutionary War, with a copy of an application for pension to prove the fact. The front page contained two sets of different names with their birthdates written later, to record the lineage of his descendants. Some of the children were born of Joseph Goings Jr., but the Joseph Goings (Goine) in the Document Number 0347 lived in Kentucky. He was not the same person who eventually lived in Hancock County, Tennessee. He was born in 1760; therefore, he was too young to be the father of the Joseph Goings of our core family of Newman's Ridge. Perhaps Joseph Goings Sr., father of Joseph Goings Jr. in our colony, was in the Revolutionary War, but I have not confirmed his participation through records at this time.

Sam Frost, son of Aletha Goings, who was the daughter of Joseph Jr., was quoted by Reverend Arthur Taylor as saying, "Joseph Sr., his great-grandfather, was in the Revolutionary War with no known details of regiments, etc." Sam Frost thought Joseph

Sam Frost, Grandson of Joseph Goings born 1840-died 1925.
Courtesy of William Grohse (deceased) Mattie Mae Grohse.

Sr. had lived in Albemarle County, Virginia.[5] His statement should be more valid than any other documentation found to date concerning any military service of Joseph Goings Sr.

Perhaps both Joseph Sr. and Joseph Jr. lived in Fairfax County, Virginia, at one time. Eventually, Joseph Jr. married Millie Lovin. Millie supposedly came from Scotland at age six (census lists Virginia) to live on a farm owned by an aunt at the site of present-day Charleston, South Carolina.[6] We do not know where Millie was born, but there were several nearby Lovin or Lovins who came

Maggie and Minnie Lovin. Courtesy of Hagan Williams (deceased)
John Williams

from across Powell Mountain on the north, into the colony. Some lived near Rose Hill, Virginia, in an area called Lovin Town, which was a cluster of homes with a spring in the center. Sources claimed the people of that area were not Melungeon, but examine the picture above of Maggie and Minnie Lovin.

Joseph Jr., a cooper, and Millie had their first child in Fairfax County, Virginia, and the second in Surry or Stokes County in North Carolina before moving to Tennessee. Historian Jack Goins places Joseph Jr. in Stokes County with John Mullins (Revolutionary War) and his son Jim prior to their living in Hancock County.[7] Jim will be discussed next in our saga of the Melungeons.

We do know from the census records that Joseph and Millie had several children, and that they both lived to be quite old. Their family, as noted in the study of the Vardy Collins family, were sometimes listed in the census as free colored and other times as white. The Goings were separated in later life and lived in separate households for a considerable period, as recorded in the census. Joseph died in 1864 in Lee County, Virginia, which is joined to Hancock County, Tennessee. The east end of Vardy Valley is divided by the state line between present-day Hancock County, Tennessee, and Lee County, Virginia.

James Mullins, a.k.a. "Irish" Jim or "Old" Jim, was supposedly born in Ireland or England in 1775-1780. He was said to be a very white trapper with a " hair lip" that was so severe he had problems smoking a pipe. He married Clara Martin, born approximately 1790 in North Carolina or Virginia, prior to coming to the Newman's Ridge area.[8] As mentioned above, reputable Rogersville historian Jack Goins ties James Mullins to his father, John, and to Joseph Goings in Stokes County, North Carolina. The country was very small at this time, and it is a possibility. A James Mullins married Margaret Walker on September 7, 1799, in New River. This might have been the same James Mullins who later married Clara Martin. "Irish Jim" was in Lee County, Virginia, by 1800 to be taxed from 1800 to 1829.[9] By 1830, Jim and Clara were living in Hawkins/Hancock County, Tennessee. A land grant is recorded in 1832 for 100 acres.

The Grohse/Taylor papers, and the Dromgoole study as well, reported the earlier Mullinses to be fair-skinned folk. They stated that after marriage into the part-Indian colony they become darker.[10] The 1830 census listed all seven in the Jim Mullins' household as free colored.[11] If Jim was "very white," the darker genes of the Martins must have been very dominant. Fortunately, we have a copy of a tintype in poor condition, of Betsy Mullins, daughter of

Jim and Clara, born in 1811-1812, below on the left. She is with her sister Nancy's (Nance) daughter, Betty, who was illegimate, and her children. Betsy married Alfred Collins, son of Vardy and Peggy. Betty, the niece, married Harrison Gibson, son of Dotson Gibson, who was killed by Confederate raiders on Newman's Ridge during the Civil War. Dotson and most others who served were listed as Union regulars, as generally north of the Clinch River in Hancock County was Union (Newman's Ridge and Vardy Valley) and Lee County, Virginia, was Confederate during the Civil War. The picture on page 161 is a continuation of the family lineage of James Mullins with granddaughter, Orpha Collins, on the right. She was the daughter of Martin and Betsy Mullins Collins. She was with her son, Lewis Collins, and his wife Sarah Gibson Collins. Orpha was married to Silas Collins, son of Solomon Collins and Gincie Goings Collins.

Betsy Mullins
Courtesy of Jo Ann Crowe

The last of our late settlers of the 1700s-early 1800s to analyze is Solomon Dickerson Collins, father of the favorite of folklore writers, Mahala Collins Mullins. The Solomon D. Collins (son) of the Tennessee area was born in 1793-1799 in North Carolina to Solomon Collins (father), who was born 1760 in Cumberland County, Pennsylvania, and Edy Dickerson. Solomon enlisted in the Revolutionary War in the Pennsylvania Line in 1777, and after being wounded, reenlisted to serve in the Virginia Line.

He was dismissed in Albemarle County, Virginia, and discharged in Richmond, Virginia. Solomon received a pension on July 9, 1819, at the rate of $8.00 per month, which was delivered to his son Robert in Lewis County, Virginia (now West Virginia). He applied

Orpha Collins
Courtesy of Phil Roberts & Johnnie Rhea & Mattie Ruth Johnson

for a bounty land warrent in Virginia in 1835, and his son George was appointed responsible for the transaction. Solomon died in Hawkins County, Tennessee, in 1838. His wife, Edy, was still living in the Hawkins County census of 1840.[12]

Solomon D. Collins married Jincie/Gincie/Virginia Goings, first-born of Joseph and Millie Lovin Goings. William Grohse reported they married in Fairfax County, Virginia. Gincie reported being born in Virginia in the census; therefore his statement seems reasonable. Solomon D. reported being born in North Carolina. The census records of the several Solomon Collins families in the early

1800s were listed only by sex and age. Therefore, they do not fit our known mix of children of either the Solomon or Solomon D. in North Carolina, although Solomon may have been in Nash County, North Carolina, in 1800. By 1810, Solomon was on the Lee County, Virginia, tax list.

Solomon D. received land grants in 1829 (Claiborn Co.), 1833, 1845, and 1845 with the last three being in Hawkins County, Tennessee. The 1830 census reported nine free colored in the Solomon D. household, with the one older female believed to be his mother, Edy Dickinson Collins.

The original house of Solomon D. was still standing on Newman's Ridge around 1990. The home had passed from Solomon and Edy, to their bachelor son and Civil War veteran, Franklin. He, in turn, willed it to Logan and Nancy Collins Mizer, his nephew and niece by marriage, who cared for him in old age. Most recently, Frank and Helen Mullins, both deceased, and their children owned the home. The log house possessed a large firplace, an upstairs with a good stairway, and an extensive kitchen on the rear with its own fireplace. The house would be very large for the early Melungeon era. If Solomon and Gincie had adequate resources, their fifteen children would certainly have justified such a structure.

Solomon Collins' Home
Ann Callahan photograph

Rumors described Solomon as a full-blooded Cherokee Indian. The Collins name does appear frequently on the Dawes Rolls and other documents as being an Indian name, but neither Solomon nor his descendants have been found on any of the listings. Some stories had Solomon fleeing outside his tribal lands as a result of conflict with the chief and unable to return for fear of death.

One of his grandsons, Ruben Mullins, migrated to Muskogee, Oklahoma, and pursued governmental payments or land grants for several years using his grandfather, Solomon, as proof of Chero-

Ruben and Elizabeth. Courtesy of Eddie Mullins & Sandra Mullins Day

kee Indian heritage. Ruben married Elizabeth Gibson before leaving Tennessee, and both he and Elizabeth were eventually involved in separate land petitions through each of their respective families. The complete series of applications and letters are on file in the National Archives. Excerpts of compensation attempts through their heritage is worth examining for insights, but there are no firm solutions into the background of Solomon.

Ruben also filed a supplemental application as an addendum to Application 2946 for his nine living children. Likewise, Elizabeth filed Application 2947 on behalf of her family lineage. Many letters ensued between Mr. Guion Miller, Special Commissioner of Indian Affairs in Washington, and Ruben over a three-year period. As Ruben could not write, the letters had different styles depending upon the author, and different degrees of etiquette or anger at composition. Some are barely comprehensible and others are fairly well written. The following pages are examples of the case.

SIR:

I hereby make application for such share as may be due me of the fund appropriated by the Act of Congress approved June 30, 1906, in accordance with the decrees of the Court of Claims of May 18, 1905, and May 28, 1906, in favor of the Eastern Cherokees. The evidence of identity is herewith subjoined.

1. State full name—

   English name: *Ruben Mullins*

   Indian name: *unknown*

2. Residence: *Muskogee, Indian Territory*

3. Town and post office: *Muskogee*

4. County: *Western District*

5. State: *Indian Territory*

6. Date and place of birth: *February, 1855, Hancock Co. Tenn.*

7. By what right do you claim to share? If you claim through more than one relative living in 1851, set forth each claim separately: *Through my grandfather (maternal) Solomon Collins (full-blood Cherokee)*

8. Are you married? *Yes*

9. Name and age of wife or husband: *Elizabeth Mullins, age 55*

10. Give names of your father and mother, and your mother's name before marriage.

    Father—English name: *John Mullins*

    Indian name: *unknown*

    Mother—English name: *Mahala (Collins) Mullins*

    Indian name: *unknown*

    Maiden name: *Mahala Collins*

11. Where were they born?

    Father: *Hancock Co. Tenn.*

    Mother: *Hancock Co. Tenn.*

12. Where did they reside in 1851, if living at that time?

    Father: *Hancock Co. Tenn.*

    Mother: *Hancock Co. Tenn.*

13. Date of death of your father and mother—

    Father: *Fall of 1900*   Mother: *Sept. 1901*

Ruben Application. National Archives

21. To expedite identification, claimants should give the full English and Indian names, if
possible, of their paternal and maternal ancestors back to 1835: _____

_____

_____

REMARKS.

(Under this head the applicant may give any additional information that he believes will assist in proving his claims.)

Solomon Collins is said to crossed into Tennessee
and married Jincy Goins, and settled there, because
he was afraid the chief would kill him if he
returned to the tribe

NOTE.—Answers should be brief but explicit; the words "Yes," "No," "Unknown," etc., may be used in cases
where applicable. Read the questions carefully.

I solemnly swear that the foregoing statements made by me are true to the best of my
knowledge and belief.

Witness to mark

willie Taylor   (Signature.) Ruben his Mullins
                                          mark
T.P. Watkins

Subscribed and sworn to before me this ___8th___ day of __November__, 1906.

My commission expires

June 30, 1910 . 190   Joshua Ross
                                          Notary Public.

AFFIDAVIT.

(The following affidavit must be sworn to by two or more witnesses who are well acquainted with the applicant.)

Personally appeared before me ___Wood Williams___ and

___W. M. Newman___ , who, being duly sworn, on oath depose and

say that they are well acquainted with ___Ruben Mullins___ , who makes the

foregoing application and statements, and have known him for 3 years and 3 years,

respectively, and know him to be the identical person he represents himself to be, and

that the statements made by him are true, to the best of their knowledge and belief, and

they have no interest whatever in his claim.

Witness to mark.   Signature of witnesses.

Wood J Williams
W. M. Newman

Subscribed and sworn to before me this 10th day of November , 1906.

My commission expires

June 1st , 1907.   [signature]
                                          Notary Public.

NOTE.—Affidavits should be made, whenever practicable, before a notary public, clerk of the court, or before
a person having a seal. If sworn to before an Indian agent or disbursing agent of the Indian service, it need not
be executed before a notary, etc.

6—421

Ruben Application. National Archives

204 So. C. St., Muskogee, Okla.,
July 20, 1909.

To Guyon Miller, Esq.;
Washington, D.C.;
Dear Sir:

In regard to the Ancestral Indian Name your requirement is unreasonable and therefore unjust.

The majority of the Eastern Cherokees never received Indian Names; and as they did not have the Cherokee written Language, they did not, (for they could not,) keep records

Ruben letter 1909-1. National Archives

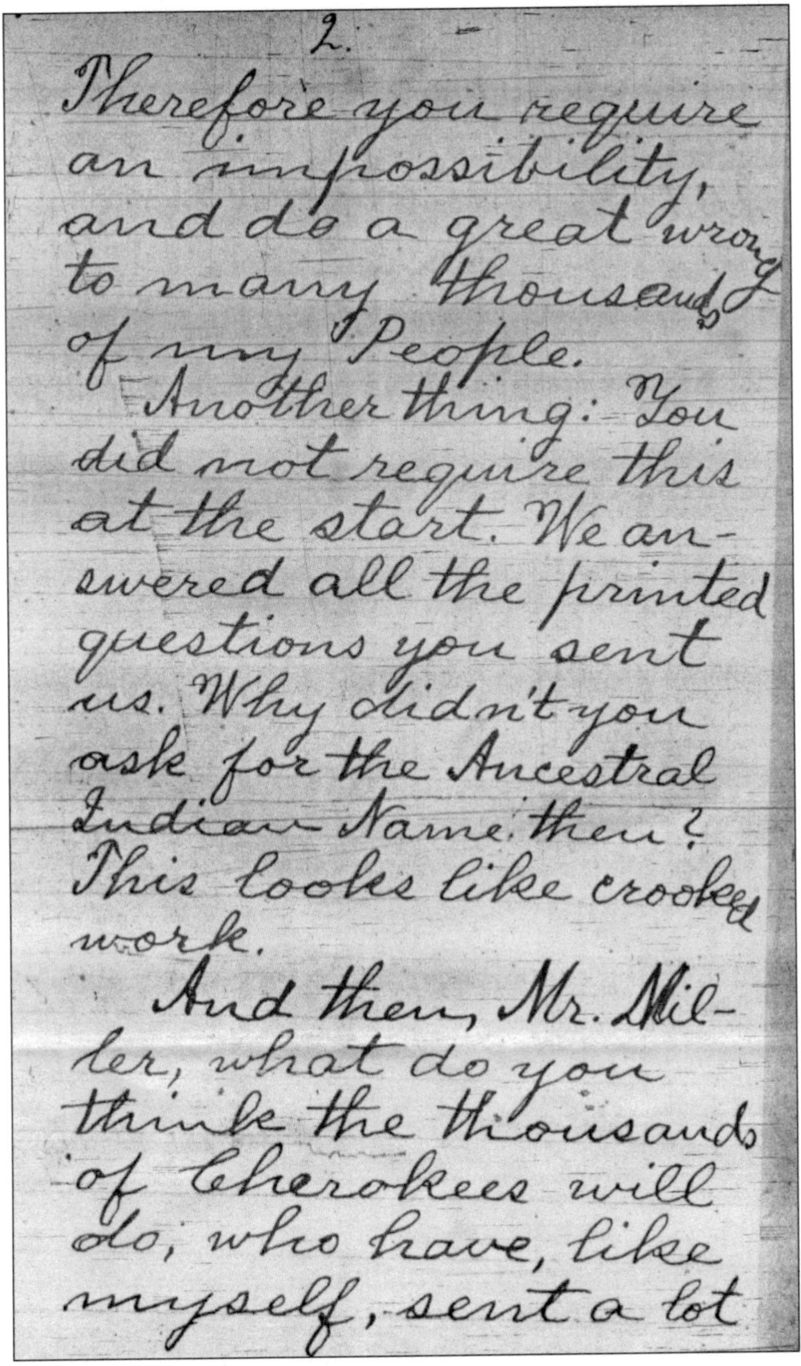

Therefore you require
an impossibility,
and do a great wrong
to many thousand
of my People.

Another thing: You
did not require this
at the start. We an-
swered all the printed
questions you sent
us. Why didn't you
ask for the Ancestral
Indian Name then?
This looks like crooked
work.

And then, Mr. Mil-
ler, what do you
think the thousands
of Cherokees will
do, who have, like
myself, sent a lot

Ruben letter 1909-2. National Archives

Ruben letter 1909-3. National Archives

A portion of Application 2497 for Elizabeth explained her logic for qualifying for compensation. Elizabeth's paternal grandparents were Joe and Susanna "Sookie" Moore Gibson. Sookie is pictured in Chapter 2 pn page 16. Joe was also known as Joe "Fisher" in the application to describe his clan name.

United States of America,)
State of Oklahoma,   ) ss.
County of Muskogee,   )

Be it remembered, that on this seventeenth day of December, In the
year of our Lord one thousand, nine hundred and seven, before me a notary
public within and for the county and state aforesaid, personally appeared
Elizabeth Mullins, of Muskogee, in said county, the applicant before the
Special Commissioner of the Court of Claims for the Eastern Cherokee Enrollment, whose application is numbered 2947, who being by me first duly sworn
according to law, doth depose and say in relation to the above-mentioned
claim as follows: My grandfather, Joe Gibson, also called "Fisher" Gibson,
lived in Lee County, Virginia, and when the Indians were driven out of Virginia, he ran away from there, and settled in Eastern Tennessee, where my
father, Keener Gibson, was born, and where my father lived during his whole
life. There was no tribal district where we lived, and no tribal rolls were
kept there, and that is the reason that we lost our enrollment. The Indian
people in that region and time were unlettered, and there was no one to instr
them in regard to keeping up their tribal relations. I have often heard my
father say that he had land in the West if he was only able to go and get it.
I was married in Tennessee and lived there until about five years ago, when
I moved to Texas, and I have never lived where I could be enrolled until
since the Cherokee rolls were closed. My grandfather could not talk English,
and spoke only the Cherokee language, and my father spoke both English and
Cherokee. Witnesses to mark   Her
minus Pearl charges   Elizabeth Mullins   mark
Wm J Belcher   X

Subscribed and sworn to before me this 17th day of December, 1907.

L. E. Naber
My Commission expires July 31, 1910.   Notary Public.
My Commission expires July 31, 1910.
My commission expires   July 31st   , 1910 .

Elizabeth Application. National Archives

— 169 —

P. L. BURLINGAME
ATTORNEY AT LAW

MUSKOGEE, OKLAHOMA June 26, 1909.

Hon Guion Miller,

　　　Special Commr. Court of Claims,

　　　　　Ouray Building, Washington, D.C.

Dear Sir:-

　　　　Your favor, notifying *Elizabeth Mullins* of the rejection
of application No. 2947 has been rejected, and of the order of the
Court of Claims in relation to exceptions in cases of rejected Eastern
Cherokee claims, was handed me for answer. Will you kindly inform me in
regard to the grounds of rejection in this case, so that I will be enabled
to advise this claimant what, if any further steps to take in the case?

　　　　By so doing you will greatly oblige,

　　　　　　Very respectfully yours,

　　　　　　　　P L Burlingame

　　　　　　　　Attorney for Claimant.

　　　　　　　Ouray Building, Washington, D.C.

Dear Sir:-

　　　　Your favor, notifying *Reuben Mullins* of the rejection
of application No. 2946 has been rejected, and of the order of the
Court of Claims in relation to exceptions in cases of rejected Eastern
Cherokee claims, was handed me for answer. Will you kindly inform me in
regard to the grounds of rejection in this case, so that I will be enabled
to advise this claimant what, if any further steps to take in the case?

　　　　By so doing you will greatly oblige,

　　　　　　Very respectfully yours,

　　　　　　　　P L Burlingame

　　　　　　　　Attorney for Claimant.

Results of Applications 2496 & 2497[14]
National Archives

This long endeavor by Solomon Collins' grandson, Ruben Mullins, does not prove anything additional in our quest for the origin of the early Melungeons in East Tennessee. It does show that he and Elizabeth were either persistant in pursuit of their heritage as Cherokee Indians living outside the area of those counted or unrelenting in their attempt to qualify for monetary gain under false pretenses.

We are fortunate to have three pictures of first generation children of Solomon and Gincie. Mahala Collins was their first born in 1824, and her myths are synonymous

Mahala with boy and girl
Courtesy of Helen Mullins (deceased)
Billie Mullins Horton

with the mystery to any astute scholar of the Melungeons. The picture is of Mahala, circa 1854, with adopted son Burton and daughter Milly/Millea. We will study her era in more detail in the next chapter.

Bailey Collins was born in 1828 and married Melissa Rhea/Ray. A son of their union, Commadore or "Bud," eventually became president of the Sneedville Bank. Martha Collins, pictured on page 89, succeeded her father "Bud" as bank president. This family was the first to come down off the Ridge and pay in gold for a good farm on the Clinch River to the dismay of white neighbors. Their payment in precious metals added to the longtime stories of counterfeiting and precision metalworking by the Melungeons.

As we recall, the metal's story has connections back to the oral reports of smelted metal by Madoc and the later searches by DeSoto for people with precious metals. The Yuchi Indians also contributed to the lore with their skills in metalwork and refining. Some metalworking and mining was also reported among the few white survivors of the Lost Colony in bondage to the Indians.

Bailey and Melissa
Courtesy of Helen Mullins

Amelia Collins – Newspaper Clip

Solomon and Gincie's daughter Pernelia, or Amelia born 1844 was married to Hamilton Miser. The picture is taken on her wedding day, March 20, 1875. Amelia and other neighbor women walked to Knoxville in 1864 to obtain supplies for local war relief. They were reported to have arrived late, and everything had been distributed. They were subsequently robbed of the few items they were able to procure on the way home to Vardy Valley by Confederate raiders. They returned home unharmed.

Thus closed the era of the first pioneer Melungeons who fled from the oppression of the colonies to the isolated area of the three-state triangle. The area was probably populated with their own kind and culture of people or, at least, by those of skin colors darker than the Eastern majority. Their visions and perceptions must have beckoned them onward with new hope for equality and rights for all on the frontier. We will leave these brave people to take a look at the new generation, some of whom are the first generation descendants of those pictured in this chapter.

---

[1]William Allen Dromgoole, "The Malungeon Tree and Its Four Branches," The Arena, June, 1891, pp. 747-750.

[2]William Grohse Papers, Latter-Day Saints Library, Rockford, Illinois

[3]Dromgoole, p. 746.

[4]Littell's *Living Age*, 20 (Jan.-March, 1849), 618-619, copy located in pamphlet file, University of Tennessee Library, Knoxville, Tennessee.

[5]Reverend Arthur Taylor Papers, compliments of Nancy Ruth Moushardt, daughter, St. Louis, Missouri.

[6]William Grohse Papers.

[7]Jack Goins Papers, Rodgersville, Tennessee.

[8]Reverend Arthur Taylor Papers.

[9]Jonesville, Virginia Courthouse, Archives.

[10]McClurg Library, Knoxville, Tennessee, 1830 census records.

[11]William Grohse Papers.

[12]ibid

[13]ibid

[14]National Archives and Records Administration, General Reference Branch, Washington, D.C., Microfilm 1104, Roll 31, Page 20, Eastern Cherokee Application Numbers 2946-2947.

Chapter 11
The Mahala Years

We'll call this period in the Melungeon era the Mahala years. Mahala Mullins was born in 1824 and died in 1898. Her large frame, which we will see in later pictures, as well as her propensity to sell moonshine throughout her life, made for many stories. The folklore and truths of her life are synonymous with many of the activities and myths of the colony of East Tennessee during the 1800s.

During an advanced period in her life, she was infected by wucheria bancrofti, a parasitic nematode worm, and developed elephantiasis, which caused an enormous enlargement of her extremities. The progression of this disease took away her mobility and added weight to the myth of her size.

Mahala and her neighbors were settled in the early part of the period. By this time, they were surrounded by a huge influx of lighter-skinned neighbors, but to them their situation did not seem too desperate. Some had good farms with substantial acreage, and others had good production, still, from the ridges. The virgin soils had not yet been depleted, and erosion had not taken its toll on the slopes.

Some activities were unique to the Melungeons, and others were typical to all living on the frontier. Life was not easy, and everyone was expected to contribute to the livelihood of the family. Children of all sizes also counted as work units (page 175) and performed daily work activities for the survival of the colony.

All during the Mahala period, the Melungeons multiplied rapidly within the confines of their limited territory; the 1830 census attested to this fact. The 55 free colored families in the county averaged six persons per family, and a fourth of the family members were under twenty-five years of age.[1] Much later studies by Pollitzer and Brown found their historical live births were still maintained at a high level. Their investigations of the 46-55 age range reported an average of 5.8 liveborn per woman.[2] Inbreeding

A work unit. Courtesy of William Grohse (deceased)
Mattie Mae Grohse

due to a limited gene pool did not seem to be detrimental, as known genetic defects have always been minimal.

Known diseases differed little from other parts of the frontier with consumption, dysentery, gout, goiter, and various heart problems being recorded. Diabetes was very prevalent in the colony and is common in many descendants today. It was usually referred to as "suga" problems or "high or low sugar" by the natives.

Men hunted deer, bear, and small game. Marksmanship was superb in the colony as perfection guaranteed food and munitions for future endeavors. Small game was also hunted. The meat was eaten, and the skins were stretched for trading with transient trappers, or, infrequently, carried to town for trade. Skins were stretched on wooden triangles called "possum" boards and hung on the outbuildings to dry. Eventually, furs were depleted locally, and the market declined nationwide. To this day, very old, mummified skins may be seen on buildings from the bygone era.

Fishing was common on the Clinch and Powell Rivers and Blackwater Creek, as well as other small streams. "Graveling" or "noodling" was practiced by reaching into the cavernous bank openings for large catfish or turtles.[3] The natives spoke of the importance of feeling gingerly for the tail of the larger turtles. They claimed the animals would not bite under water, but that concept is not logical to the feeding and survival of the turtle. Large fish were sometimes found deep in the river under logs or in caverns. Men would dive, attach a rope through the gills of a large fish, and wrestle it to the surface. Eventually, depleted resources and loss of creative motivation led to netting, traps, and dynamite. The Zur Pond, centrally located atop the Ridge, provided many fish as well as facilities for washing, prior to the repeated use of explosives for fishing. The pond finally developed cracks and the waters were lost forever into the aquifer.

The women and children gleaned the many native plants of the area. Spring brought "bears lettuce," "branch lettuce," or water cress from the many small streams and creek banks. It was frequently eaten raw with a liberal application of salt.[4] They picked pails of wild "shallet" greens such as polk, narrow dock, crow's feet cress, lambs-quarters, and the many other plants they knew to be edible. They cooked the many varieties of greens with a small piece of salt pork. Hard corn-pone was a popular accompaniment made with yellow or white corn.[5] Berries were available for eating or selling in town. Long-term food preservation did not seem to be a significant part of the culture.

The Dry Zur Pond.
Courtesy of Ann Callahan.

Ginseng was hunted in the fall as a cash crop. Areas of ginseng were known, and top prongs were carefully harvested when the larger roots with two to four prongs were present. Some conservation was practiced but mostly respected due to the market demand for the larger growth. Even at this early period in our history, the Orient was a market for the supposed aphrodisiac.[6] The root is still harvested in the area today and sold by the pound. A recent local buyer was overhead telling, "I'm gettin excited gist weigen up this sang for shippin!"

The Melungeons didn't use ginseng because it was too expensive to waste on themselves, but they did have many superstitions and cures of the woods. Many were common on the frontier, and others were unique to their clan. They used goldenseal, dogwood, and sassafras bark for stomach problems. Slippery elm bark was used for boils and infections. Ratsvein was for heart problems and ground ivy for thrush.[7] Perhaps their agriculturally oriented lifestyle and dependence upon the basics of nature contributed to a very complex use of many remedies not necessary or known to the general population.

A superstitious belief in witches was prevalent. Ransoms for their goodwill was symbolized in the form of a coin in milk, a butcher knife cutting through milk, or salt in the fire as payment to rid witches from a churn. Even imagined frog-shaped markings on a person's body meant the presence of witches and a concern for all the colony. [8] "Charmers" were found among them. They could rub away warts or moles for a small fee. One woman supposedly possessed "blood beads" that "wair bounter heal all manner o' blood ailments."[9]

A knife under the bed of a pregnant woman would cut the pain of delivery. A howling dog, and they had so many that human feces deposited outside their simple homes was one of the animals limited sources of nourishment, meant a death would occur soon. A red bird in the morning was a bad omen for the shedding of blood. Many activities were done by the signs of the moon, as well as all of the crop planting.[10]

Superstitions and herbal cures were not solely Melungeon activities, and neither have ceased, even with continued and progressive improvements in education. Many of these practices were not fatal. This could not be said for other events in their lives. One of the key occurrences came with the Tennessee legislation of 1834.

Let us follow the law changes leading to the disenfranchisement of the Melungeons. These events were mentioned earlier but need to be reviewed and elaborated upon in order to recognize their overall importance.

In 1794, the state had declared that "all Negroes, Indians, Mulattos, and all persons of mixed blood, descended from Negro or Indian ancestors to the third generation inclusive, whether bond or free, to be incapable in law to be witnesses in any case whatsoever, except against each other, no person, thus disqualified, can be a witness, in a State prosecution, for a defendant who belongs to one of the disqualified classes."[11]

This law was followed with a law in 1796 declaring, "every freeman of the age of twenty-one and upward being allow to vote. Being an inhabitant of the state and resident of one county of the state six months preceding the day of election, shall be entitled to vote for members of the general assembly, for the county in which he shall reside." Freeman included free Negro, and in the case of Melungeons, free colored.[12]

In 1834, the Tennessee law was changed again, taking away privileges of the free colored, stating, "Every free white man, of the age of twenty-one years, being a citizen of the United States, and a citizen of the county wherein he may offer his vote, six months preceding the day of election, shall be entitled to vote for members of the general assembly and other civil officers, for the county or district in which he resides." Free men of color were exempt from military duty in time of peace, and also from paying a free poll tax.[13]

This law remained in effect until the Civil War.

This law also reduced the flow of Melungeons from North Carolina and other states to Tennessee, because prior to 1834, they were allowed to vote in Tennessee but not in their previous home state.[14] Even though the law allowed them to vote prior to this time as "polls" in the tax lists, they were often challenged as having an unidentifiable portion of Negro blood. Trials were often held to determine by flatfootedness whether a Melungeon was allowed to vote. Flatfooted meant "free colored" and not eligible to vote, while some arch meant enough white blood for sufferage.[15]

The long-term significance of this law was its legislation of inequality. James Aswell painted an oversimplified but depressing picture of the new situation after the law of 1834. The newcomers had a legal right to oust the squatters. The Melungeons could have been killed, one by one, illegally from ambush, but that method was far too slow. Aswell stated that another added disadvantage to those who coveted their possessions lay in the fact that the Melungeons would have been more than their match at ambushing.

He continued, "Suddenly, the Melungeons discovered that the white strangers they had watched, with but little anxiety, settle among them in significant numbers were, cow-bird like, pushing them out. They were driven up the ridges or onto other poor land that was undesirable to the victors." Early in the period, many had larger land grants, but acreage diminished while productive fertility levels were lost.

The Melungeons did not accept their loss meekly and hoped for a future. Against that day, they nursed their hatred, and their day began with the firing on Fort Sumter. Excuses for guerrilla activities became common during the chaos of the middle period of the 1800s. Throughout the Civil War, bands of them roamed East Tennessee raiding, looting, burning, and killing. "Melungeon" was no longer a synonym for outcast. It meant terror to the adversarial white neighbors.

At the end of the war, the Melungeons returned to their unproductive areas to live. The people in control soon forgot the lawlessness of the period. It would have been sheer suicide to send troops into some of the areas, for only a few could have used their skills of the woods to frustrate a small army.[16] We must remember this period was chaotic and a time for all to reevaluate the goals and stability of the country. By this time, the Melungeons were back in their secluded areas and were rapidly losing the potential for any new opportunities that might have developed with the uncertainty of the times.

We should examine this same epic era written later in a more colorful and discriminatory manner by Brewton Berry: "Early in the last century, when the white folks first come here the Melungeons was already here, ahold all the good land in the creek bottoms. The white folks was covetous of that good land, but don't want to just take from the Melungeons brutal-like. Well, it wouldn't a' been no trouble if the Melungeons was ordinary heathen Indians. They woulda' just kicked 'em out. But here they was sorta' livin' like civilized folks, and they was speakin' English, an' on top o' all that they was believin' Christians. But their skins was brown on account o' their Injun blood. So the white folks begin sayin' they had nigger blood in 'em too. Then they passed a law sayin' nobody with nigger blood could vote, or hold office, or testify in court. Then they went to court and before long they got hold o' that good bottom land. So there wasn't nothin' left for the Melungeons to do but move up on the ridges."[17]

This version of the deteriorating situation of overcrowding bigotry is recounted in this version by Berry, a writer of the 60s. Today's reader can still wrestle with the humor and feel the sadness and inequality.

The repercussions from the legislation of inequality were far-reaching. For a group that had tried to have their own culture and identity, it was unacceptable to them to be lumped with Negroes and be treated as Negroes, who, at the time were like second-class citizens.

Education was an example. Little formal education was present in the county prior to the Civil War. The first schools in Hancock County were subscription schools, where parents were charged a fee to support the teacher and maintain the building, often the local church building. With the limited funds in the community, school was not a priority.

When public school funds were mandated in 1873, a Negro public school was located at Sandy Flats on top of Newman's Ridge.

Melungeons did not attend this separate, but so-called, equal school.[18] In fact, this type of forced integration resulted in their hardly attending a school of any type in rebellion to the mandate.

Let us examine another series of key activities that led to the decline of the Melungeons. The making of various types of alcohol was common on the frontier, and the Melungeons were not oblivious to its potential for income. The distillation of grain into alcohol was an easy way to solve transportation problems, as well as raise the price per bushel of their limited harvests of grain. The government was aware of this situation, and they and the individual states had passed various laws to attempt to control the manufacture and sale of illegal alcoholic beverages.

Laws were passed by various states through the early period of the 1800s, with some adopting total prohibition by the 1850s. This was difficult to enforce, and most of the states returned to the licensing method of regulation. During the Civil War, federal licensing resumed in order to raise wartime revenues. In 1866, licensing was abolished for strictly excise payments.[19]

Though regulated, many people in the remote areas made and sold alcoholic beverages with limited risks of varying physical or financial harassments from the law. The end result was that successful violators avoided the excise tax, and penalties were generally only minor, such as the destruction of production equipment or court appearances with a small fine.

Some historians feel the Melungeons' involvement in the making of alcohol has been exaggerated, as have so many of their other cultural activities. The people who believe this must not know the history of the Melungeons of Newman's Ridge. The first question my mother asked after learning of my initial trip to Tennessee was, "Jimmie, did you see all them stills up and down that ridge?" She did not realize she had left fifty years before and the economy had changed. She only remembered that her and her neighbors' migration to Indiana led to changes for them, while to her, Vardy must have remained forever the same. In spite of potential opportunities, she also knew that some neighbors came to Indiana only to revert to their known vocation of making moonshine in a new market area.

The federal court held in Knoxville, Tennessee, listed various and multiple times these violators of the revenue lawscame before the court. The following members of just the Collins family were: Batey, Benjamin, Braham, Calloway, Conaway, Duncan, Elcaney, Floyd, Harrison, Hillery, Howard, Jerry, Joe, Bud, Bailey, John, Landon, Larkin, and others. Some fines were low, consisting of only court costs, while others were $10 to $100 up to $1,000. Some were dismissed with no costs. The Collins family was not unique in distilling liquors. The Mullinses competed with them and many other neighbors for the business. Wayman, John, John Jr., Joseph, Larkin, and others were arrested and paid fines in Knoxville Federal Court, ranging from $10 to $200.[20] The Gibsons, Stewarts, Misers, and others also found the business to be important for their survival.

Eventually, vast amounts of liquor to produce, to hold on inventory, and to sell contributed to their own decline. The daily temptation was too readily available to ease their misery. This seems to be an all-encompassing statement, as not all Melungeons were participants in the business of illegal liquor, but the activity was so rampant within the colony that it had a detrimental effect on the very soul of their culture. For example, my grandfather, as far as is known, did not have a still, but one of his sons was involved in the business. He was eventually sentenced to life imprisonment in Michigan City, Indiana.

Let us return to the families on the ridge for further analysis. We know little of Mahala Mullinses husband, Johnnie (Skinney), but family members say he was so good with a knife that competitors would try to slip off with any new knife he procured to attempt to break out the blade. He once said, "I'm so tough I been knifed, shot, and the Lord hit me with a thunderbolt so hard he knocked my shoes clean off and I'm still here."[21]

Folklore runs more rampant in this area with his wife, Mahala Mullins, reining as the "Queen of the Moonshiners." She was active in the business, and her unhealthy weight contributed to the embellishment of the stories, allowing writers great creativity in the area of exaggeration. She was always large in frame and weight. In the picture on page 183, circa 1863, she appears as mother to Rubin, Ollie, and Calvin (her last-born and my great-grandfather). Her weight at this time would probably have been 300 pounds. She was approximately 39 years of age and not yet noticeably infected with elephantiasis.

The stories say that the law would infrequently go up the long trail to her home to either imbibe or serve her with a warrant for arrest. Both statements were true. Upon the announced arrival of a lawman, she would go to the door laughing and try to squeeze her 800 pounds through the door. Each time, the deputy would return to the jail with his warrant and slam it on the table in frustration. Eventually, there was a backlog of seven warrants issued for her arrest when Wash Eads was elected sheriff. He personally took the seven warrants to her home to

Mahala with sons
Courtesy of Ellen Bales Link

establish his credibility as the new chief lawman of the county. Mahala again laughed as the sheriff pondered aloud the possibility of tearing the house down. She reprimanded him for even thinking of such an activity. She responded, "The law don't allow you to tear down the house, Sheriff Eads!" Her comment prompted Sheriff Eads to turn over his newest and last warrant and write across the back: "Mahaley Mullins—catchable, but not fetchable."[22]

Another story told of a picnic near the Powell River supported by a politician running for Congress. After the free rabbit stew and beer, the picnikers were asked to participate in a wrestling contest. Of course, Mahala appeared, and they all laughed with, "Wrestling's for men!" at the prospect of her fighting. Black Joe Bascom challenged her by saying, "Take heed, wench! I'm a-coming at you!" The dust flew, and it sounded as if someone was beating carpets and driving stobs, but not for long. The dust settled, and the form wrapped around the tree trunk, limp and unconscious, was Black Joe Bascom.

The story continued as Mahala took on two wrestlers at once, then three, and finally four, one from each side. Finally, all the contestants were in a pile as she stood before the judge, chewing tobacco vigorously, to claim her prize. She replied, "Yo're giving a fat shoat for the prize, ain't you?" She has a special request; in lieu of the shoat, she wants to sell moonshine in gourds resembling a primitive canteen. With his approval, she calls out, "Peeg! Peeg! Peeg!" and seven of her dark and barefoot bucks (husbands) came out of the woods with a supply of gourds. The judge tried to renege on his offer when he found the gourds did not have an excise stamp, but relented when Mahala challenged his promise.

When the judge heard she had seven husbands he screamed, "Bigamy." Mahala responded, "I was only sixteen last year when I took seven husbands. Now I'm seventeen and got my full growth and now a-lookin for a few more good husbands. Spread the word!"

From then on, people took notice of that Melungeon-bred woman, and the moonshine business accelerated for Mahala way up on Newman's Ridge. By the next year, the first drove of deputies scaled the cliffs and sheer walls to Mahala's for an arrest, but to no avail. Others followed for six to fifteen years, trying to retrieve her for arrest. Usually, they only destroyed her mash receptacle and left in frustration.

Finally, the chief of all the revenuers in Washington heard of the ongoing embarrassment and led a special team of twenty-two men toward the encampment of "Big Mahaley." The story sounds as if they are scaling Mt. Everest as they blasted, drove stakes, and prepared a route to retrieve the aggravation on the ridge.

When they finally met her at the door in her big rocking chair, she offered them a gourd of her "best likker to sup" while she heard of their great attempt to retrieve her from the mountain. They refused the "likker," and she challenged them to move her down the mountain.

The leader told of their one big post and a block and tackle. He said, "We aim to let you down off this ridge in a big rope sling and then cart you from the cliff bottom in a wagon."

Mahala responds, "Well now, that sounds like a right smart notion. Did you think of that all by yoreself?"

"Well, no ma'am, not quite all by myself," said the leader agent. "Some of the little details was thought out by others. But mostly it's my own figgerment."

The story ends at last with the men unable to retrieve her, and by law, she was legally protected from their doing any damage to her home. She died twenty or so years later, and the big post for

Mahala at the Barrel. Courtesy of Thomas & Rebba Zachary.

the block and tackle, along with the other work done by the revenuers helped the thirty-three husbands and fourteen cousins move her to her grave through an opening in the wall.[23]

The fact is she had been too large to go through her doors for several years. She was also immobile during this time, as elephantiasis had taken its toll on her legs. She and her family were fined frequently, but neither she nor the lawmen were able to take her to court.

Some of the true stories of the Mahala period seem almost as unreal and tragic as those of the above folklore. Near the end of Mahala's life, her boys were drinking heavily and they argued over a woman. We know that brother Elby was home, along with Calvin (my great-grandfather), mother Mahala, and her nephew Willie Davidson, son of Gib and Sally Mullins Davidson. Calvin was a heavy drinker and was upset over possible infidelity between his wife "Coose" (see picture on page 202) and his nephew Willie Davidson. Willie was lame in one leg and always hopped, in lieu of using crutches or a cane. He was obviously not a physical match for Calvin. Calvin accused Willie of having an affair with his wife and chased him out the rear door with a shotgun. The chase was brief, as Willie hopped and had little hope of fleeing the onslaught of the swifter Calvin. Calvin caught him with the butt of his shotgun to the side of his head with such force as to knock his eye out of the socket. Willie went down, temporarily blinded in one eye and partially conscious. Calvin leaped on for the kill and commenced to strangle the remaining life from the breathless Willie. Willie was just conscious enough to draw his .38 and discharge it into the chest area of his adversary.

Stories say Mahala watched the event, noticed their abandoned drinks, and commented after the tragedy, "I can't let this good shine go to waste, I'll just drink it myself." Calvin lay dead, and Willie survived to stand trial and be acquitted. The judgment was that he had acted in self-defense. Secondly, he was judged a cripple and credits were given for him being at a disadvantage. "Coose" abandoned her three children: Hattie (author's grandmother) to equal time spent between Grandmothers Mahala and Haines and Mary Ann Mullins Miser, Bob to Larkin and Sarah Collins (Aunt Tony) Mullins, and Frank (page 188) to John Jr. and Julia Ann Gibson Mullins.

"Coose" disappeared after the death of Calvin for a long period before reappearing with her new children, Charlie and Virgie. She eventually married Dolcy Minor, and the children were named Charlie and Virgie Minor. Below is daughter Hattie and son Frank (page 188) followed by Charlie (page 189) and Virgie (page 190) born of "Coose" Mullins and an unknown suitor after Calvin was shot by Willie Davidson.

Willie Davidson married twice and sired many children before dying at an old age. He never regained sight in the dislodged eyeball. He wore a black patch over the eye and continued to hop with the characteristic gait the rest of his life.[24]

No doubt, this true story was embellished with the comments by Mahala. As for the judgments on the character of Calvin Mullins and Willie Davidson, they were both considered to be bad citizens of that era. Calvin had been arrested many times for revenue and firearms violations. He drank heavily and became belligerent to the point of fighting frequently. Willie, his nephew, did such inhumane acts as setting a bed afire with a person in it to prove to the occupant of the bed that he was a hypochondriac. He once offered to delouse a neighbor's mule, doused it with gasoline, and set it on fire. The mule died before the fire could be extenguished.[25]

Hattie Mullins Bales. Courtesy of Hattie Bales (deceased)

Frank Mullins. Courtesy of Hattie Bales (deceased)

Charlie Minor. Courtesy of Hattie Kinsler Collins.

Virgie Minor Kinsler. Courtesy of Abe Kinsler

Several of Mahala's children did survive to adulthood, in spite of the overall decline of health and conditions within the colony. The firstborn, Jane, born in 1841 when Mahala was 17 years of age, prospered with her marriage to Howard Collins, grandson of Vardy Collins.

Jane Mullins.
Courtesy of Helen Mullins (deceased)
Billie Mullins Horton

Jane, above right, is with daughter Docia Collins on the left and daughter Kyrie next to her. Kyrie, who married Tennessee Goins, has Flora, Mollie, and Julie at her side with Mathis and Lillie. Mathis was eventually shot and killed in the school entrance by Sheriff Wardell Collins. Note the large physical stature of these family members compared to Docia, previously shown on page 154 alongside her father, "Big" Howard Collins.

Burton (below) born 1846, was not really a son of Mahala, but

Burton Mullins. Courtesy of Helen Mullins (deceased)
Billie Mullins Horton

was raised by her. Burton, born of Sarah Gibson and Lon Taylor, was adopted by Mahala when Sarah was working as Mahala's caretaker. Burton married Lillie Sizemore, who is pictured. Lillie was the daughter of Sis Mary and Tivis Sizemore. Sis Mary was the daughter of Bailey and Melissa Rhea Collins (on page 172). Bailey was a brother to Mahala. Burton died in Camp Nelson in the Civil War.

No known pictures exist of Elbe, born 1848, but his son Lath, born 1872, is pictured below with wife Eliza Massengill (Gibson). He later married Sarah Gibson, sister to Eliza.

Mary Ann was born in 1853 (on page 200) and John Mullins, Jr. was born next in 1855. John married Julia Ann Gibson, and after her

Lath Mullins. Courtesy of Frank Mullins (deceased)
Billie Mullins Horton

death, he married Maggie Lovins. The Lovins came from Rose Hill, Virginia, across Powell Mountain. Pictures and descriptions show them to be dark skinned, with black eyes and hair. They socialized with the Newman's Ridge people by crossing Powell's Mountain on horseback, which was approximately a five-mile trip.

John Mullins Jr.
Courtesy of John Mullins III
(deceased) Aileen Mullins

John, born 1855, is pictured with Maggie Lovins and son John Mullins III, who died recently. He was the last living grandson of Mahala Mullins. In the picture, John, Jr. is 60 years of age and Maggie, a twin to Minnie, is 21 years (page 158).

John Mullins, Jr. was a good citizen as well as prosperous and lived to be 70 years of age. His home, now called the Martin house, still stands on the Panther Creek Road. He had two sons, John III and Ernest Kyle. John III was warm and friendly throughout his years. Brother Ernest Kyle innocently got mixed up in my Uncle Connor's escape from the Tennessee State Prison, and spent a few years in prison himself.

Little Johnny Mullins III (deceased)
Aileen Mullins

Ruben Mullins. Courtesy of Eddie Mullins & Sandra Day Mullins

Ruben, born 1856, was discussed and illustrated (page 163) in Chapter 10 as he and Elizabeth went to Muskogee, Oklahoma, to pursue Cherokee Indian lands. They were never successful in their attempts, and their descendants still live in Muskogee.

Calvin was the youngest, born in 1860 and was shot in 1895 by Willie Davidson, as enumerated above. The last surviving picture burned in a fire at the home of his daughter, Hattie Mullins Bales, but he looked and acted very much like his grandson, Carnell Bales. Except for a small goatee, Carnell was also similiar to his grandfather, Calvin, in temperament. He graduated from high school in uniform and went immediately to World War II. He served in the infantry and swam off the beach to be rescued by a ship, as he survived the first ill-fated invasion of the Philippines. During his return and participation in the occupation of the Philippines, he frequently celebrated to excess with many other battle-fatigued veterans. During a drunken ride in the back of the truck with some white and Negro enlistees, one Negro looked at him and said, "Us niggers have got to stick together." Carnell responded with, "I ain't no g — d — - nigger." The other Negroes in the truck attacked Carnell and threw him out for dead. He was found the next day, semiconscious, with one ear almost torn off. He recovered and served until the end of the war.[26] Carnell died in mid-adulthood of what was diagnosed as lupus.

No known pictures exist of the other children of Mahala and Johnnie who survived early childhood. The others were Sally, born 1843; Larkin, 1844; Millie, 1846; Elbe, 1851; Richard, 1852, a twin whose sister died at birth. Richard died a violent death as his gun misfired in a brawl, and his throat was slit before he was thrown in a well. Jerry was born in 1854 and Ollie in 1859. He was shot in 1882 in downtown Sneedville by the sheriff, Grant Jarvis. Lewis was born in 1859 and Calvin in 1860.

The examples given here, with an emphasis on the Mullins family, show them to be in a state of decline and decadence. The Mullins clan was neither the best of the colony nor were they the worst. As for their economic resources, they were better-off financially than most due to their volume in the sales of illicit liquor.

Carnell Bales, Grandson of Calvin Mullins. Courtesy of Carnell Bales (deceased) Cornice Bales

Will Allen Dromgoole wrote of the people living in miserable hovels with few windows or just openings for doors or windows. She told of them hanging a quilt up to the door openings to keep out the cold. She reported them sleeping on straw, and not very clean straw, for bedding. She said they had no windows or candles; therefore, they retired with the departure of daylight. Many were said to have slept on the bare ground. Others were to have shared their cabins with domesticated animals or have animals underneath the elevated foor.[27]

Many people consider this type of reporting by Dromgoole to be discriminatory against Melungeons. The skeptics consider her work mostly fabrications, but denial and rationalizations are reasons for our ignorance of the many injustices in which our forefathers participated without leaving us with feelings of guilt. Perhaps

Dromgoole was prejudiced and projected her feelings in her writings, but do we really believe she fabricated the entire story of the Melungeons? Was her motive in studying the culture of these people to write falsehoods? Even if her writings were partial truths, the Melungeons were in a state of poverty at the time of her studies. We will see later that this was the end of their period of decline.

Let's look at some houses of the era which are still standing today. The examples are all houses of my family, but they will give us an idea of the Melungeon abodes. These particular homes were all better than those described by Dromgoole, but there were many that would fit her descriptions.

Since we are still exploring the Mahala period, we'll look at Mahala and Johnnie Mullin's home, which is still standing on Newman's Ridge (page 197). The house was rebuilt after being burned by Confederate raiders in 1862-63. This house and the first home were frequent stopovers for buyers of illicit liquor made by the Mullins family. Bartering was common, and Mahala and family seemed to have a large inventory of material goods accepted for liquor. Guns, skillets, pots, knives, ammunition and other items were in abundance at the home. So, during the Civil War, raids were frequent in the area of Mahala's house. The Confederates were only one mile down Vardy Valley in Lee County, Virginia, and always knew of the potential for supplies at Mahala's.

One story tells of the Confederate raiders coming to loot and kill the Mullins boys and their kin home from the Union Army. Jane (Mullins) Collins (page 191), wife of Howard Collins (page 154), spotted the raiders first and screamed, "The Rebs." Howard Collins and the other Union soldiers on the premises took shots and then jumped the bluff at the spring, as the Confederates crouched to attempt to analyze the numbers of the resistance. The Rebs advanced, but their adversaries escaped down the ravine by the spring. Howard Collins sustained a broken leg in the assault.

The raiders set the house on fire after looting and departed. The family hurriedly worked the conveyor bucket connected to the spring to extinguish the fire and restore order. Some of the children were still very young. Calvin, the last born and my great-grandfather, was an infant. No sooner had the fire been extinguished, than the raiders returned and ordered all outside into the light skiff of snow. The children were barefooted. Calvin was carried by sister Mary Ann (page 200) on her hip, as she was a small girl. This time the Confederates torched the house and waited with the family to watch it burn beyond salvaging before departure.

As the raiders were descending Newman's Ridge, Johnnie Mullins overloaded his gun and left the ramrod in because he was very angry and distressed over the calamity to his family. He fired, split the barrel, and lodged the ramrod in a rail fence down in the valley.[28] The story ends as a second house was built which still stands today for our examination.

This home was of good construction with decorative arches over the front windows. Downstairs was a fireplace, living-area room, and separate kitchen. A stairway led to a full loft upstairs for sleeping. Approximately 500 square feet upstairs and 500 square feet down made this a generous-sized house for the period. Even though Mahala and Johnnie raised fifteen children to adulthood with six dead in infancy, the span of births was long, and some were gone before others were using living space. This Melungeon family would have been considered prosperous due to their lucrative business of the distillation and sales of alcohol.

The last known residents of the home were Hughie and Laura

Mahala Mullins's Home. Photography by Ann Callahan.

*Huey Mullins's Family. Courtesy of Carl and Betty Mullins Hilton &
R.C. and Macie Mullins*

Mullins and family (above) who purchased the property after
World War II with earnings from work in the shipyards of Maryland.

Another house of the Mahala period was the Carson and Ellen
Bales Stewart home. They were more recent residents, living in the
home in the early 1900s. The basic home is of, and symbolizes, the
earlier period. Carson was the son of Jim and Laura Collins Stewart.
Laura was the daughter of Howard Collins and Jane Mullins
Collins. Ellen was the daughter of Bob and Hattie Mullins Bales and
one of the few blond, blue-eyed Melungeons of the area. Hattie
and Laura were first cousins. This home is now a small storage
shed, and had one room with low ceilings. There were probably 300

square feet of living area in the one room.

Carson and Ellen divorced, and both were eventually remarried. Carson moved to a different home and ran a very prosperous liquor business by piping a spring line under his second home to support two large storage tanks. He transported the liquor over a large territory, and once arrogantly told a neighbor, "I've been farther under the bed to get my pot than you've ever been anywhere in your life."[29]

Carson & Ellen Bales Stewart's Home
Photograph by Ann Callahan

Carson Stewart
Courtesy of Howard Stewart

Ellen Bales Stewart
Courtesy of Ellen Bales Stewart Link

Haynes and Mary Ann Mullins Miser Home.
Photography by Ann Callahan

The Haynes and Mary Ann Mullins Miser home was on the forks of the road from Vardy Valley over Newman's Ridge to Panther Creek, called "Panter" Creek by the natives even today. Mary Ann was the daughter of Mahala and Johnnie Mullins and Haynes was son of Hamilton and Amelia Collins Miser (page 172), sister to Mahala. Hamilton was the son of the first Miser in the valley known as "Old" George Miser and Prudence Mullins Miser, daughter of "Irish" Jim Mullins. Haynes and Mary Ann were not the first residents of this home, but it had two floors and a fireplace with approximately 250 square feet on each floor. In the mid 1990s, the house was sold for the logs and moved out of the state.

Mary Ann Collins Miser. Courtesy of Hattie Mullins Bales (deceased)

The age of the Dolsey and Francis "Coose" Martin Mullins Minor (pictured on page 202) home is

Boat to Dolsey and Coose's Home. Courtesy of Hattie Bales (deceased).

unknown, but older residents say as long as they can remember it stood on the other side of the Clinch River. The homesite could only be reached by skiff. It washed away with the floods of the 1950s, but a hand rope still crosses the river at the site. A more recent home is currently hidden up the ravine from the river.

The home resembled the Dromgoole descriptions, with no true windows except for holes and only a semblance of a door. The dwelling had around 500 square feet and a fireplace for heat and cooking. The elevation allowed pigs, chickens, and dogs to find refuge under the house. The animals could be observed and heard through the cracks in the flooring. "Coose," widow of Calvin Mullins, eventually lived in the home with Dolsey Minor. She chewed tobacco and could spit out the window opening with great accuracy. She also smoked tobacco in clay pipes said to be made by her own hands. "Coose" walked everywhere and carried a .38 caliber revolver in her bag throughout her life in preparation for a future confrontation with Willie Davidson. Fortunately, their paths never crossed. The gun is still in the family and was last seen in the possession of her youngest child, Charlie, (page 189) who was born in 1903 to "Coose" and an unknown father.

The last home to consider is one structure placed over the deceased. The Melungeons had several interesting burial customs which probably were not unique to them, except for their grave sites. Mourning lasted for two-three days with socializing, courting, and drinking the latest recipes. The people were very emotional,

Dolsey & Coose Home. Courtesy of Hattie Mullins Bales (deceased).

and wailing would ring over to the distant hills. The body was usually carried to a family cemetery where all walked in a long, single, processional row to the final resting place. Naturally, there were Collins', Mullins', and Gibson cemetaries, which were all quite large, as the people were very prolific. The unique, small houses built over the graves are one of the mysteries of the group. The Eskimo members of the Russian Orthodox Church in Alaska are the only known people who build such small villages over their burial areas.[30] They used the miniaturized houses, at times, for hiding illegal whiskey.

Melungeon Grave Cover.
Photography by Ann Callahan.

As we examine the Melungeons, we see many of the familiar characteristics of a people in any isolated subculture. They were particularly similar to the many small pockets in Appalachia. They believed in individualism, traditionalism, self-reliance, and religious fundamentalism. The one big difference from their Appalachian neighbors was their disadvantage of being distinguished as Melungeons.[31]

What causes an isolate to behave in a manner different than the norm? Richard Ball stated that "one cannot comprehend the behavior of Southern Appalachians by assuming all human behavior is rational, for the stubborn recalcitrance of the mountaineer simply resists explanation in these terms. Most observers cannot easily understand the daily experience of inexorable pressure, 'insoluble problems', and absolutely overwhelming frustration that are the daily experiences of the poor."[32] These words accurately describe the evolving condition of the Melungeons in this period.

This period ends with Mahala infirmed and old with the ravages of elephantiasis. She has lost Johnnie and her will to compete with the pressures of discrimination right along with her people. She still sat in the big chair by the kitchen window waiting for customers to taste her brew, but as she peered out and thought of the sorrows, of the violent and tragic losses of Burton, Richard, Ollie, and Calvin, life did not seem good. She still had some of her family nearby to manage the business. Her granddaughter Hattie, abandoned by her mother after her father's tragic death, spent most of her time tending to her grandmother. With assistance, Hattie religiously helped lift her onto the galvanized tub with 4x4 cross members for bathroom activities. Hattie remembered her during this time as still patient and gentle, but a reflective grandmother. The ravages of many family deaths and confrontations with the law must have been almost too much for her to bear. As she had never professed

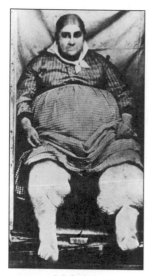

Mahala's
Elephantaesis
Courtesy of Hattie Bales
(deceased)

a faith in Christianity, she had little spiritual hope to sustain her, as her ways and those of her people were rapidly being challenged by the material needs of their neighbors. By this time, their big land grants were diminished, and their marginal lands were declining in productivity.

Mahala died on September 10, 1898, just as the beauty of the ridge begin to show its fall colors. The family dismantled an area of the house where a fireplace was to be and enclosed the sides of her bed into a makeshift coffin. Colony members walked or rode horses back for miles to congregate, drink "shine," and mourn her passing. A large number of pallbearers carried her

> Obituary of
> Mahaly Mullins
> was borned March the 30
> 1824 Deceast September
> the 10 + 1898
> Age 74 years 5 months and
> 10 Days She profest faith
> in Christ a while before her
> Deth and Called for Gohney
> and Rutin to give ther
> hands that they wold meet
> thur in heven She told
> Stephen Gibson if She
> was never permited to
> Shake his hand in the
> world She wold Shake
> hands with him on the other
> Shore

Mahala's Obituary.
Courtesy of Eddie Mullins & Sandra Mullins Day

Mullins Cemetery. Photography by Ann Callahan.

huge diseased body (probably 500-600 pounds) to the family site to join Johnnie, Ollie, Calvin, Millie, Coffee, and other members of the clan. Before primitive stone markers were removed to prevent vandalism, at least sixteen unmarked stones could still be seen in the family cemetery. Only the site of daughter Millie/Millea could be identified by the writing on her stone. Mahala's original tattered obituary is in the possession of the descendants of Ruben Mullins in Oklahoma.

As we reflect on the stories of this critical period in the evolution of the Melungeons, we see a people being enveloped, isolated, and failing to compete in the ongoing contest for resources in the human race. Karl Mannheim theorized that, "A closed society fosters the same meaning of words, the same ways of deducting ideas, inculcated from childhood on into every member of the group, until divergent thought processes cannot exist in that society."[33] They lost whatever oral and unwritten heritage they had because they were being called Melungeons, which they reject to this day. Increasingly, they were being called free colored, mulatto, and linked with Negroes. In this period, Negroes were certainly treated subserviently by whites in control, and those dropped into this cate-

Mahala's Grave. Identified by Hughie Mullins (deceased).

gory would be depressed and demoralized.

In the end, legislation took their rights and, eventually, their education. Moonshine extended their longevity in the hills, but captured their souls as they succumbed to the temptations it offered. They were at the bottom of their civilized cycle, but do we see hope on the horizon?

[1]Jean Patterson Bible, *Melungeons: Yesterday and Today*, Rodgersville, Tennessee: East Tennessee Printing Company, 1975.

[2]William S. Pollitzer and William H. Brown, "Survey of Demography, Anthropometry, and Genetics in the Melungeons of Tennessee: An Isolate of Hybrid Origin In Process of Dissolution," Human Biology, September 1969, Vol 41, No. 3.

[3]Phyllis Barr Thesis, "The History of the Melungeons," East Tennessee State, Johnson City, Tennessee, 1965, p. 29.

[4]ibid

[5]Bonnie Ball, "The Melungeons", Historical Sketches by the Historical Society of Southwest Virginia, No. 2, 1970, pp. 64-65.

[6]Phyllis Barr, p. 34.

[7]ibid, p. 29

[8]Will Allen Dromgoole, "The Malungeons,' The Arena, Volume 3, March 1891, Boston, Ma., p. 476.

[9]Mildred Haun, *The Hawk's Done Gone*, New York, New York, The Merrill

Company, 1940, p. 75.

[10]Phyllis Barr

[11]Meigs Tennessee Supreme Court Reports, Volume 1, 1832, p. 119.

[12]Constitution of Tennessee, annotated by Robert T. Shannon, Nashville: 1915, pp. 374-375.

[13]ibid

[14]J. W. Caldwell, *Studies in the Constitutional History of Tennessee*, 2nd Edition, Cincinnati, 1907, p.148.

[15]Swan M. Burnett, "Notes on the Melungeons," American Anthropologist, Volume 11, p.348.

[16]James Aswell, "Lost Tribes of Tennessee's Mountains," Nashville Banner, August, 22, 1937.

[17]Brewton Berry, *Almost White*, New York, MacMillan & Company, 1963, pp.17-18.

[18]Harry M. Caudill,"O Appalachia!" Intellectual Digest, Annual edition April 1973.

[19]P. R. Collier and Sons, *Colliers Encyclopedia*, New York, New York, 1955, Vol. 16, p. 373.

[20]William Grohse Papers, Latter-Day Saints Library, Salt Lake City, Utah.

[21]Reverend Arthur Taylor Papers, Latter-Day Saints Library, Rockford, Illinois.

[22]Vic Weale, "Home folks," *Knoxville Journal*, July 24, 1951.

[23]James R. Aswell, *God Bless The Devil*, The University of Tennessee Press, Knoxville, Tennessee, 1985.

[24]Interview with Frank Mullins, son of Lath who was son of Elby who witnessed the tragedy.

[25]Interview with Hughie Mullins, whose Grandmother was Nancy Collins Mullins,Mullins, Davidson (wife of Willie).

[26]Interview with Carnell Bales.

[27]Will Allen Dromgoole, "The Malungeons", The Arena, 3 March 1891, 470-479.

[28]Interview with John Mullins III (deceased), Knoxville, Tennessee, last living grandson of Mahala Mullins, & William Grohse papers, Latter-Day Saints Library, Rockford, Illinois.

[29]Interview with Ellen Bales Stewart Link.

[30]Louise Davis, "Mystery of the Melungeons," *The Nashville Tennessean Magazine*, September 29, 1963, p.16.

[31]Thomas Q. Zachary, "The Malungeons-A Review of History and Change", University of Tennessee, May, 1972.

[32]Richard A. Ball, "A Poverty Case: The Analgesic Subculture of the Southern Appalachians," American Sociological Review, 1968 extrapolated from Thomas Zachary papers

[33]Karl Mannheim, *Ideology and Utopia*. New York: Harcort, Brace and World, 1936.

Chapter 12
The Missionaries Cometh

In 1891, Will Allen Dromgoole said, "They are exceedingly illiterate, none of them being able to read. I found one school among them, taught by an old Malungeon, whose literary accomplishments amounted to a meager knowledge of the alphabet and the spelling of words. Yet, he was very earnest, and called lustily to the "chillering" to "spry up," and to "learn the book."[1]

Until the Civil War, no public or private schools existed in the area. An occasional roving tutor would pass through and work for room, board, and a small sum of money, but few could afford such a luxury. Even though many of these people were called teachers, with credentials of a fifth grade education from a "civilized" section of Tennessee or neighboring Virginia, they could contribute little to the education of their students.[2] The mandate of public school funds in 1873 did little for their situation because the Sandy Flat school on Newman's Ridge was for Negroes, and the Melungeons were legally expected to go to school at Sandy Flats. They refused to enter the premises of a school with such criteria.[3]

At the end of the last chapter, there was hope that someone would come from over the mountain to save and enlighten a lost people. A distant church sensed the calling as two Presbyterian missionaries, Dr. Christopher Humble and gospel singer Dr. Snodgrass, were traveling and investigating in the area in 1892.[4] There is certainly some suspicion that this area had problems known in far distant places and that these people were more than random passersby. History tells us the men, by chance, came through the valley and dropped in upon a church meeting at the Old Sulphur Springs Baptist Church.

The introductory meeting seemed productive and led to yet a bigger meeting at the Collins boarding house, where the missionaries would inform the people of their desire to educate the colony and win souls to Christ.[5]

The first meeting seemed workable, and the Presbyterian Missionary Board decided to send two single women into the foray of the unknown in the midst of the Melungeons. Miss Margaret McCall, a Washburn College graduate from Topeka, Kansas, and Miss Annie Breem Miller of Rogersville, Tennessee, were chosen. The mix was good, for McCall was an outsider and a Northerner, and Miller lived just south of the Melungeon area, but, no doubt, had some educated expectations from the suspicious and isolated people.

The young women were to establish Sunday Schools and convert the people to Christianity. They were to promote awareness in the value of education with the offer of free training to any and all who desired to pursue new opportunities.[6]

Miss McCall related: "We were the first workers there, rode the same horse together, visited in the many cabin homes together, and had many pleasurable and pioneer experiences...

"They made moonshine whiskey and had 'blind tigers' there and felt that they could not send a man worker there, but only women. My father came down and put us up a cabin...He made a house with one large room where we could have Christian Education Meetings, and a kitchen and two small bedrooms (dirt floors). We had school one day a week, Sunday School, and visited in the homes. Before I left, we had two Sunday Schools in our valley and two over Newman's Ridge on Panther Creek, and one on the ridge on Thursday. Nancy Collins was our constant friend, and through her, we got over our messages about not liking people to stand outside the windows and spit tobacco juice inside, about washing dishes in clean water, and about drying them..."[7]

We are speculating as to why two young girls were sent in the first wave on this monumental task to revive the colony, but they do mention "blind tigers." Probably, the vast amount of illegal liquor being processed would arouse the local population's suspicion toward an outside man as either a revenuer or potential competitor. Women did not normally engage in liquor production, only in sales, if at all. Another possibility of the selection of two girls is that some the men of the colony were promiscuous with willing partners, but in their culture the men were not known to be rapists; therefore, the girls would be relatively safe. Anybody known to force themselves on a woman could be shot by vigilantes or unknown assailants and thrown into the tall weeds.[8]

The church and the school remained closely connected as the Presbyterians successfully pushed for the saving of souls and free education for all who responded. Within a short period, McCall and Miller were

Nancy Collins Miser
Courtesy of Cecil Miser & Polly Horton Miser.
Nancy is pictured on the left and also in the
picture on page 151, bottom, on the left.

having some successes, and a bigger school and church were needed. A mission house served their immediate needs along with the school, but the prospects were improving the potential for a larger facility.

The new Presbyterian church was started in 1898 and finished in 1899, with 25 charter members. Shortly afterward, this structure led to a series of mission stations in the area; One in Snake Hollow

1st Vardy School 1880-1902. Courtesy of William Grohse (deceased)
Mattie Mae Grohse

Vardy Mission House 1890s.
Courtesy of William Grohse (deceased)
Mattie Mae Grohse

(west end of Vardy Valley), one in Ebenezer (between Vardy and Sneedville), and one on the Clinch River (on Dr. Mitchell's land). In addition, a church was built in Sneedville, and the McKinney Academy, a Baptist school, was transferred to Union Presbytery, Presbyterian Church U.S.A. as a missionary, three-year high school. Many of its students eventually came over from the Blackwater-Newman's Ridge area.[9]

The church cost less than $2,500 to build, and the money came from a grant of the office of the Presbyterian Church of New York. Following their long-range strategic plan, some labor, lumber, and materials came from the community.

Vardy Presbyterian Church.
Courtesy of Saturday Evening Post

Miss Maggie Miller remained in the system. She and Miss Maggie Axtell were assigned to be superintendents of Sunday School and to missionary work under Reverend J. H. Wallin. Two new elders were elected, with Noah Collins and Ardell Collins being chosen. Munlus Collins was the first deacon.

Noah Collins
Courtesy of Mary Edith Collins Sympson (deceased)
Wayne Sympson

Noah pictured with his wife, Alice Lovin Bales Collins (my great-grandmother), Charlie, Vardy, and Mary Edith Collins. Noah married Alice Lovin Bales after her first husband, Gilmore Morgan Bales, was found shot and floating face downward, in the Powell River. Gilmore and Alice were from the Rose Hill area and had only one child, Robert, my grandfather. Robert was orphaned after his father's death.

Munlas Collins.
Courtesy of Isa Mae Collins McCay (deceased)
C.M. (Jerry) Collins

Pictured here are the first deacon, Munlas, 30 years, and Fluie Horton Collins, 19 years, on their wedding day in 1905. Fluie was fair, with red hair and freckles. Previously, Munlas had seen her barefoot in her yard as he walked the Vardy Road. He finally developed enough courage to stop and knock on her door with a suitor gift of a pair of shoes. She threw the shoes into his face and slammed the door. Later she reconsidered.[10]

In this closed society, it is interesting to note the names of the charter members of the new Vardy Presbyterian Church. They were: Larkin Collins, Rachel Collins, Caney Collins, Darthula Collins, Kit Collins, Magdalene Collins, Wardell Collins, Frankie Collins, Shelby Williams, Tom Anderson, Tom Jenkins (working in Collins' boarding house), Baty Collins, Noah Collins, Alice Collins, Munlas Collins, Tennessee Goins, Cary Goins, Docia Collins, Jane Collins, Hattie Mullins, Clay Miser, Nancy Miser, and etc.[11]

In 1900, the Women's Association of the Presbyterian Church, U.S.A. responded with money, and the church provided the teachers with a new school. The building was 26x20 with one room and three windows on a side. Blackboards were painted on every avail-

2nd Vardy School.
Courtesy of Scott Collins

able wall space. A six-foot stage was in the rear of the building. The ceiling was tongue and groove lumber. The double floor was supported with 2x12 joists for the strength to handle the toughest of student traffic. The bell tower tolled and echoed throughout the valley as a beckoning call for the new opportunity to educate oneself out of poverty. By 1902, there were 25 students, by 1913, enrollment was 65. The curriculum suited the needs of all the people, with basic and preparatory courses, along with agriculture, industrial arts, hygiene, and homemaking.[12]

The progress was slow, but the people responded. The Presbyterians made them feel good about themselves.[13] They had not been treated with respect for a long time. The word Melungeon, and its connotations, was a despised term, and this word was not being used by their new benefactors. As an added bonus, the white neighbors were not even coveting their newly found salvation or competing in their progress, for their resources for education were coming from an outside church. The county's limited resources were not being shared with these isolated citizens; therefore, adversaries ignored or were unaware of their neighbors' opportunities for spiritual and mental growth.

Baptism in the Clinch.
Courtesy of John Mullins 111 (deceased)
Aileen Mullins

Going to Church.
Courtesy of Hughie and Laura Mullins (deceased)
R.C. and Macie Mullins & Carl and Betty Mullins Hilton

The union between the church and the people continued to work as just the right personalities had been sent to mesh with the Melungeons. At different times, dissenters would challenge the missionaries, but they were relentless in their faith and plodded onward toward their vision of saving souls with free education for all.

By 1910, Miss Rankin had come to Vardy and stayed on for 34 years. Gloria Frady wrote of her: "Miss Rankin taught all ages during weekdays, and preached Sunday School to the parents and children alike on the Sabboth. She set up a school lunch program and friends helped prepare a nutritious hot meal every day. The older children would take turns doing the dishes and cleaning up afterwards. As time went on, she offered a night school to the farmers and they came respectfully in handfuls, swallowing their pride, and they all learned to read and write."[14]

Miss Rankin Responding to the Bell.
Courtesy of Helen Mullins (deceased)
Billie Mullins Horton

Mary J. Rankin.
Courtesy of Martha Collins (deceased)
Georgie Collins Wetherred

Miss Rankin was born in Scotland, raised in Minnesota, and college educated, which was a first for the local system. Even though she was of Scottish descent, it seems probable that her dark features were probably a Presbytery qualification for her mission. Her working arrangement was approved by the Hancock Board of Education. She received $25.00 a month, with $6.00 for incidentals plus a box of crayons. For those more affluent, she added a charge of two extra months of tuition at twenty-five cents per month. Parents with less funds were allowed to work for the extra tuition.[15] She worked faithfully and eventually retired in 1944.

We cannot talk of this period without touching upon Arthur Taylor. His father, grandfather, two uncles, and a brother were all Presbyterian ministers.[16] Even though he was a short-term seminary student during his tenure in the valley, his impact was significant. We don't know if the seminary or the church, if either, asked him to study the genealogy of the Melungeons of the area, but he did so diligently. Fortunately, there were still living survivors who could remember those of the past during his time in the area. He studied and recorded many of the older oral family histories that are still being reviewed today. He also fell in love with and married one of the local Melungeon girls during his limited stay in the area.

Arthur married Grace Miser as pictured opposite with their family. The Miser family was large (see on page 210 parents Logan and Nancy Collins Miser). William Grohse, which was the later local historian of Vardy and has researched extensively for many statements in this study, married a sister to Grace Miser Taylor. The complete genealogical studies of Reverend Arthur Taylor were eventually given to William Grohse, his brother-in-law, for posterity. Grohse preserved them and continued the studies that are now on microfilm in many major libraries. These two men single-handedly recorded much of the early and later heritage of the colony of Newman's Ridge. The work is not without error, but their pioneer-

Reverend Arthur Taylor.
Courtesy Nancy Ruth
Taylor Maushardt

ing research has prevented many of these ever elusive people from being totally lost to the history of the colony.

Reverend Taylor was truly a devout Christian man. Not only was he an excellent writer with a pungent, homey, original, down-to-earth style, but he was also very determined and inflexible in his beliefs. He wrote newspaper articles for many years with the explicit rule that none were to be censored. Reverend Taylor was firm in his convictions and never compromised when God's work was questioned. He hated the use of tobacco and liquor, and he never hesitated to say so.[17] One wonders how he survived the many trips up the remote paths to visit ridge people with such uncompromising values. They must have admired his grit and sincerity because he attempted to recognize them as equal and to pursue their friendship.

Perhaps his greatest legacy was to help relocate many Melungeons to Southern Illinois, where he spent most of his years in the ministry in the Alton and Cairo Presbyteries. Whether by church plan, Arthur Taylor plan, or chance, many migrated to the area to work in the bakery and shoe factory of Chester, Illinois. Menard Correctional Center also provided opportunities for some of the people. Once they knew of these new opportunities beyond Hancock County, they branched out to many other new areas.[18]

Optimism continued to improve. The Presbyterians fostered a sense of pride and hope in the forsaken people. For the first time since their loss of identity, some began to understand themselves and their capabilities, and they were beginning to yearn for something better than that of their forefathers. Their hopes moved to an even higher level on May 5, 1920, when Chester F. Leonard arrived to preach in the church and be principal in the school. He was handicapped by his poor health, his superstitions of the people, and the unwillingness of some to pursue an education for their children. However, he made up for all these problems because he was a believer, and he was doggedly persistent.

Chester Leonard had been born a poor boy, but scored highly enough on tests to be able to attend Northwestern University in Evanston, Illinois, and to graduate with honors. He went on to McCormick Seminary and graduated in the same year as his first assignment in Vardy Valley, 1920. He was well aware of his new challenges, as he had spent one summer of seminary among the people of Vardy before graduation. The school was growing, and there was suddenly another new infusion of inspiration to the entire community!

Mr. Leonard and his new bride, Josephine, traveled those final miles by the popular mode of transportation of the area, two mules and a buggy, with nervous and inspired guidance from the Lord. The creaking wheels led to a tireless accomplishment for the pair in the knowledge of grain, poultry, gardening, teaching, preaching, homemaking, and whatever other activity they felt needed or enlightened to pursue. Every day, Mr. Leonard was to function as a husband, headmaster, teacher, coach, mechanic, plumber, pastor, leader, and friend. Josephine was right alongside him as wife, cook, organizer, hygienist, encourager, appreciator, diplomat, and a general spreader of sweetness.[19]

Road to Vardy 1920s.
Courtesy of Ellen Bales Stewart Link

By 1926, Reverend Leonard understood the need for a larger school and presented a new proposal to the community leaders. They unimanously concurred, and Logan and Nancy Miser deeded four acres of land for the school property on January 5, 1929.

As in the past, this was planned as a joint project. The Board of National Missions of the Presbyterian Church, U.S.A. donated the necessary cash for the building. The community was to donate, cut, and drag the logs to a staging area by mule, as well as saw and stack for drying all 60,000 board feet of lumber. Every able and cooperative citizen was recruited for lumber donations and processing. Logan and Nancy Miser, Dan Horton, Herbie Collins, Bob Bales, Connor Bales, and others donated lumber. Everybody worked, including a few females. Ollie Bales, a young, tomboyish teenager, dragged the cut logs from the woods to the sawyers with a team of mules. She recalls the period with, "I drug them logs outa the wood, and there weran't no women round." She paused. "You know I mighta been raped after all them days in the woods." Then she added, "Them men didn't rape neighbors; they'da been shot!"[20]

The school, and what a school it was, was ready for the 1929-30 school term (below).

Vardy School.
Courtesy of Vardy Historical Society. (Original Glass Slide)

The 1899 church is in the foreground, and the new 1929 school is in the background. The school had three levels: the basement, first floor classrooms including an auditorium, second floor teacher's rooms, with a library and museum. All levels could be reached from the ground level. Excellent facilities were available, and they were utilized for all the needs of 150 students and staff.

The school even had a modern kitchen for serving hot lunches and learning homemaking skills. This complete program had evolved from students bringing their own lunch to the church and the school sharing some food supplies. The new lunch was not free, as a small fee was expected. Those who could not afford the fee usually provided some labor by the father for maintenance or cleaning. The basic premise, that people must learn responsibility in order to become self-sufficient, was in the background of every decision.

Along with the kitchen, the school had a shop for industrial arts and woodworking, a science laboratory, an extensive library, dormitories for students and teachers needing lodging, and a night school for adult education.[21] Nursing care was always available,

Entrance to School.
Courtesy of Drew and Alyce Williams (deceased)
Druanna Williams Overbay

Gladys Miser and Mrs. Leonard.
Courtesy of Gladys Miser Feegle

and various outside company representatives were scheduled to lecture on products that would enlighten the sheltered and isolated people. This school provided for all needs for the progress of the community no matter how complicated or insignificant the problems appeared to be.

Mrs. Leonard (above) and her husband were parents of Chester Leonard and worked for periods in the complex. The picture is of Gladys Miser shown on page 17 as an adult. In response to the picture, Gladys said that people really did not utilize their sewing skills because clothes were always supplied by the missionaries from New York.[22]

The entire school concept, with its extensive recreational facilities became an exemplary model of perfection in East Tennessee, and educators came from all around to study the facilities and discuss its administration with the staff. Reverend Leonard personally recorded the weather, inoculations, diseases, attendance, honor roll, weight gains, and height growth for every student. The records are fascinating to read, as he logs deaths, births, snake meetings at various nearby churches, shootings, and even attacks upon his own person. He notes on May 25, 1936, "Tennessee Goins and Simeon jump me in the woods at night-try blackmail."[23] Hope, opportunities, and behavior patterns were definitely improving in the colony, but even with such hope and opportunities, a few were reluctant to receive the message. After being so low, it was difficult for some to pull themselves back up to humanness. Illegal alcohol production and its negative side effects were still very prevalent among the populace.

Reverend Leonard Classroom.
Courtesy of Ellen Stewart Trent (deceased) David Trent

Reverend Leonard never relented as he pursued his dream for his people. People from considerable distances beyond Vardy knew of his works and would smile and·repeat accolades of his great accomplishments when his name was mentioned. Mr. Leonard took time to communicate the good news with people beyond the colony. He was unstoppable in his efforts to improve the overall conditions of his people.

In one newspaper communication, he spoke of the need for better roads in the area. He said roads were needed for children who

The Playground Trolly.
Courtesy of Helen Mullins (deceased) Billie Mullins Horton

Recreation for all.
Courtesy of Drew and Alyce Williams (deceased)
Druanna Overbay

walked up to four miles on rocky paths, and for people from all over the county to use to access the extensive four-acre playground in the rear of the school. He spoke of the need for roads for fine school privileges, for more students from longer distances who might be too fatigued to study from walking, and for better health care. The health care issue was prompted by the difficulty of outside medical doctors to get to the colony, and, when present, their neglect of additional patients due to fatigue.

Mr. Leonard also said that roads would enable one to get to know neighbors. He specifically mentioned the county seat of Sneedville as an example of how, through roads, they could know the Vardy community as friends and neighbors, instead of depending upon rumors and stories for their judgments. He even reiterated the economic losses to the county for lack of a road from Sneedville to Vardy as he spoke of $21,000 of goods used by the church system, all brought down the Vardy Valley from Virginia, which resulted in funds lost to the county.

A road was not built over Newman's Ridge to connect Vardy with the county seat of Sneedville until the early 1930s. My mother, who left Vardy in 1932 and never revisited, was amazed that I could traverse over Newman's Ridge to Vardy by car in 1980. She could only envision riding a horse across the mountain. During this same discussion, she spoke of old horses, no longer able to carry their riders over the ridge, were subsequently shot on the spot with a revolver. She said, "We'd shoot 'em rite tween the eyes, an leve 'um fer the buzzards."[24]

In spite of the poor infrastructure, including no electricity in homes until after World War II, the school and the people progressed socially, economically, and morally. The people learned of new worlds, attractive Melungeon women were selected by outsiders for marriage,[25] and jobs developed with the new awareness and educational qualifications that have been prerequisites for movement away from Vardy.

People were influenced by the missionaries to move to distant places. Once a family became established in a new area, friends and relatives were close behind. Education, motivation, and hope with Christian love were the ingredients of a new success story.

All did not work out perfectly. Some individuals were too far

Vardy Store 1940.
Courtesy of Macey Mullins

gone to save. We should mention one or two people who could not handle this wonderful gift of the missionaries and their hope for a new and better life for the people of Vardy. During one Christmas season, Mathis Goins humiliated and forced Mr. Leonard to climb the large cedar Christmas tree in the church. Mathis was eventually shot and killed, at an early age, by Deputy Wardell Collins in the narthex of the church.

Another lost soul was Patton Gibson. The Bob Bales family migrated to Indiana with the Dan Hortons, Ely Fleeners, Carson Stewarts, the Gene Mullins, the Sizemores, and several Collins families. Bob's move was influenced by Chester Leonard and enticed by Patton Gibson's comments of, "There's so many dollars en Indyany! Hit almost grows on the trees!" The Bales family migrated to near Salem, Indiana, to join a new colony, and Bob bought the farm of Patton Gibson, son of Shepard. Patton was considered a shrewd businessman, but seemed outwardly laid back and friendly. He carried the devious reputation of having six notches on his .45 and carrying six equal silver dollars in his pocket as a record of his lifetime of murders, but he was kin.

Patton exposed his true character in the transactions leading up to sale of his Indiana farm to his old neighbor from back home. The barn mow was full of loose, moldy hay that was unfit for livestock feed. He covered the entire moldy mass with a new and thin layer of fresh hay in order to get full financial benefit from his inferior inventory. This devious effort was discovered later.

Patton also spoke of his prosperous sawmill behind the barn to be an extra incentive for buying the property. He conjectured the mill would pay for the farm with lumber sales, besides extra money from custom sawing for neighbors. After possession, Bob Bales did not find the local market to be accepting of rough-sawn timber as many of the local sawers already had a monopoly in the area. In a short period of time, the mill was abandoned for lack of sales.

Later, Bob Bales found fifty-gallon barrels of abandoned moonshine buried in the sawdust of the sawmill behind the barn. Patton's volume of sales must have been very high for him to have forgotten entire barrels of finished product. Patton did speak truthfully when he sold the sawmill as a working mill, but he failed to qualify the word working.

Eventually, Patton's luck ran out, and he was surrounded and shot on the farm by John and Pleas Spurlock in revenge for his earlier killing of their father in Virginia. The Spurlocks were jailed in Salem, Indiana, and within the week, four sons of Patton stormed the jail to attempt to kill the Spurlocks. Sheriff Milt Trinkle and his wife were both shot in the leg as the sheriff stalled for time in his efforts to deny the keys to the Spurlock cellblock. The Spurlock boys barricaded the cell door and nervously waited in the dark as the Gibsons frantically hunted the keys. Meanwhile, Odie Gibson stood guard outside while the unarmed citizens of the small town gathered with the fire department and watched in horror.

The town marshal, Elmer Geralde, finally arrived at the scene. The marshal and Odie scuffled on the porch and rolled down the steps before Odie was able to draw his weapon and shoot the marshal. His first and only shot was not fatal, and the marshal was able to retaliate with three shots of his own. Odie was dead. The marshal was critical, and the brothers inside could not find the keys. The Gibsons fled the jail without revenge, and a massive manhunt began. A posse was formed, and armed men searched Jackson and its adjoining counties. One brother escaped to Tennessee, but was finally found in Virginia and extradited for trial in Indiana. The Bales and Callahan (new Bales son-in-law) families attended all the legal proceedings and trials in shame for these people were kinfolk. Their mental situation was not good, because they had recently relocated among strangers. These people with fragile self-worth perceived that they carried the same stigma because of their association with their fallen kin, who were always outside the mainstream of the community.

The Gibsons were eventually all buried in Vardy, including Patton. His corpse was returned with all the pretentious trappings, as well as the biggest marble marker that could be purchased with liquor profits. He had rings, watches, and some say, the silver dollars in his pocket for each man he had killed. The night after his funeral, he was dug up by the local citizens and relieved of all his unneeded and salable possessions. He was quietly and carefully returned to the grave before daybreak, and nobody has ever told of the incident outside a select circle of confidants.[26] One wonders if the notched gun will ever surface as an oddity of the lost era.

We cannot leave the fallen without visiting Uncle Connor, the oldest son of Robert and Hattie Mullins Bales and brother to my mother. Connor, who had ambushed and knifed a teacher after a paddling in the second grade, did not fare any better than Patton at his new home in Indiana. He continued to work the illegal whiskey business with two other transplants, Johnny Collins and Carson Stewart. They worked in the stone quarries of the area by day and in their distilleries by night. The trio were even so brazen as to drive the roads in search of barrels to steal. When one was sighted, the bravest would proceed to the porch, dump the water, and carry it to the truck in broad daylight. Apparently, no homeowners felt brave enough to challenge their bold and daring activities.

Connor could not overcome his earlier environment as he continued along the wrong path. Numerous sentences and paroles were the vocations of his entire life. On one occasion, he escaped from the Tennessee State Penitentiary, stole a car in Indiana, and returned to Tennessee to "lay low" from the law. This became a bigger offense than some he had committed up to this time, because the transportation of a stolen vehicle across state lines was a federal offense, and the F.B.I. was involved.

Connor drove the stolen car to the home of Johnny Mullins, Jr. to visit with cousins Johnny III and Earnest Kyle. He spent several uneventful days enjoying their hospitality and activities around their farm. They were good and unsuspecting hosts, and Connor could be a delightful guest. Meanwhile, his father, Bob Bales, had returned to Tennessee from Indiana to try to find his wayward son. He loved Connor, as any father would, in spite of his long history of crime. He just did not know where to look for him in Tennessee, as most everyone in the colony was kin and a potential for his hideaway; besides, communication was very primitive in the area in 1930s.

Connor soon tired of the daily visits with the cousins and suggested they go to Sneedville with him for some fun. Innocent and unaware, Earnest Kyle departed with Connor in the stolen car for the county seat. They had hardly stepped out onto the street when Connor noticed a rather loose-knit, large group of strange-looking men posted in several strategic places throughout the small town. They did not look like the locals. Connor whispered to Earnest Kyle to head toward the car as he drew his revolver. The gun prompted several of the F.B.I. to draw weapons and yell, "Stop, you're under arrest!" Connor discharged his gun at the head of the nearest suitor. Luckily, the shot only pierced his hat. In spite of the volleys of gunfire, Connor and Earnest Kyle were able to get to the car and head out of town toward Panther Creek with the F.B.I. in hot pursuit. Earnest Kyle was petrified and lay unconsoled on the floorboard. Connor performed to the best of his ability as he led them on a chase that is still remembered as the biggest event ever on Panther Creek.

Toward the Virginia line, a tire was hit, and Connor abandoned the car and ran toward the mountain, en route to Virginia. Poor, trembling Earnest Kyle was retrieved from the car and arrested. Connor knew the territory and evaded all attempts of arrest as he fled up the narrow paths toward Virginia. He stopped briefly enough to hold up a small store for ammunition before proceeding up the mountain. As luck would have it, the storekeeper had a phone and called the police. A posse ambushed Connor at the state line. He surrendered with no resistance and was sentenced to Levenworth, Kansas. Earnest Kyle was sentenced to prison for a shorter sentence as an accessory to the crime.

Connor was eventually sentenced to life as a habitual criminal in Michigan City, Indiana. After a few years, he became ill with cirrhosis and liver cancer and was moved to Methodist Hospital in Indianapolis. He was near death, and even in this state, he was surrounded by armed officers and handcuffed to the bed. He died shortly after and was buried at Brownstown, Indiana, at age 49.[27] Why was he so evil? Could he have been saved if he had lived in a better environment during his formative years, or would he have been evil in even what we call a normal society?

Connor Bales in Vardy (third from right).
Courtesy of William Grohse (deceased)
Mattie Mae Grohse

Connor Bales.
Courtesy of Carnell Bales (deceased)
Clarice Bales

Connor and Jimmie.
(Author -Jim Callahan)

Everybody enjoys reading about wild and violent people, but the entire point can be missed if we only focus on the bad. The haze of hopelessness and despair had diseased these people like a malignant cancer in the late 1800s and now a cure had been found in the form of the missionaries. Lawlessness continued to be bad, but the people had hope.

There were other Mathis Goinses, Patton Gibsons, and Connor Baleses, but there were many more who were achieving success in the world under a code of morals and ethics.

By 1952, the colony as a whole was progressing and dispersing. The session of the church met and was confronted with a resignation request by Moderator Leonard. It was his desire to resign from the Vardy Church. He left the room and turned the meeting over to Elder Drew Williams.

A sorrowful discussion ensued with session members reiterating the desire of the membership to retain Reverend Leonard, but accepting his resignation with the following statements:

1. It is the sincere desire of the interested members of the church for Mr. Leonard to remain as their pastor and leader of the community.

2. Their pride in Mr. Leonard for conducting the only church in the county with a regular worship service and for its message, which is carried throughout the county.

3. Their appreciation for Mr. Leonard's direction and leadership in the school which is a model for all of East Tennessee. Visited by noted educators to study the equipment, playground and the curriculum.

4. His management of the healthcare of their people year after year. His plans and enaction of the reduction of the spread of diseases. His skills in procuring medicines, bandages, and first aid.

5. His raising of the level of the life of the community through work in the church, school, health, and regular community meet-

ings on Friday and many other special meetings.

6. Again let it be said that it is the sincere desire of the people of Vardy Community that Mr. Leonard stay with us as our leader.

Mr. Leonard was called back to the meeting and took over AGAIN as moderator.

Elder Bell closed with prayer.[28]

Mr. Leonard was touched by the love of the people and joy of carrying on God's work in Vardy. He stayed on another five years. Meanwhile, education, marriage, and time all contributed to the steady migrations out of the valley to such places as Chester, Illinois; Baltimore, Maryland, and Gary and Salem, Indiana.

The school remained in operation until 1973 when a lack of funds for repairs and declining attendance caused the facility to be closed. The remaining students of the community were bused to Hancock Elementary School in Sneedville.[29]

End of an Era.
Photography by
Ann Callahan

[1]Will Allen Dromgoole, "The Malungeons." The Arena, Volume 3, March 1891. Boston, Ma., p. 477.

[2]William P. Grohse, *History of Education in the Vardy-Newman's Ridge Area*, Hancock County, Tennessee, June 28, 1971.

[3]Danny Hugh Turnmire, "Education of the Melungeons," From Distinction to Extinction.", Union College Thesis, Barbourville, Kentucky, August, 1984, p. 21.

[4]Grohse, ibid.

[5]Jimmy G. Mathis, "History of Education in Hancock County", Unpublished reports presented to Education Department, Lincoln Memorial University, Harrogate, Tennessee, 1982, p. 12.

[6]Mathis ibid, p. 14.

[7]Mathis ibid, pp. 12-13.

[8]Interview with Ollie Bales, daughter of Robert and Hattie Mullins Bales.

[9]Grohse, p. 2.

[10]Interview with daughter of Munlas and Fluie, Isa Mae McCay, Baltimore, Maryland (deceased) & C.M. Collins.

[11]William P. Grohse, *First Vardy Presbyterian Church U.S.A. Record Book*, Vardy, Tennessee, 1899.

[12]William P. Grohse,"Echoes from Vardy ", Hancock County Post, February 2, 1976, p. 4.

[13]Interview with W. C. Collins, Sneedville, Tennessee.

[14]Gloria Frady, "She Went into the Hills to Do What Was Needed." The State, Columbia, South Carolina, Feb. 3, 1974.

[15]Grohse, p. 3.

[16]Arthur Hamilton Taylor Obituary 1884-1949.

[17]John A. File, "A Man of God ", Newspaper article, source unknown.

[18]Interview with Cecil Miser, son of Logan and Nancy Collins Miser, Sneedville, Tennessee.

[19]Amelia Burr Elmore, Family Portrait, Source Unknown, Her Interview with Oppie Miser on the Road to Vardy.

[20]Interview with Ollie Bales Callahan. (Mother of author).

[21]Danny Hugh Turnmier, p. 23.

[22]Interview with Gladys Miser Feegle.

[23]Reverend Chester Leonard and Vardy Church School Records, McClurg Library, Knoxville, Tennessee.

[24]Ollie Bales Callahan.

[25]Henry Price, *Melungeons: The vanishing Colony of Newman's Ridge*, Hancock County Drama Association, Rogersville, Tennessee, 1971.

[26]Papers of Arthur Taylor, *The Salem Republican-Leader December*, 1930-October 21,1931, Interviews with Hattie Mullins Bales and confidential witness to exhumation of Patton Gibson in Vardy.

[27]Interviews with Johnny Mullins III and Bobby Bell Kinsler.

[28]William P. Grohse, Minutes of Session of 1945 Vardy Prebytery Church.

[29]Danny Hugh Turnmier, p. 24.

Chapter 13
The Aftermath

What has happened to these people who might have been the first boat people to America? What happened to this group of people who battled discrimination throughout their American history only to falter during the 19th century, and then regain new hope with the coming of the missionaries in the late 1800s? They are now approximately 50 years past the retirement of Reverend Chester Leonard.

Outside factors have led to the dissolution of what we have identified as the colony of Newman's Ridge. With this we have lost many worthy individuals as well as their unique culture and history. We live today, look forward to tomorrow, but we learn from yesterday. We must not lose our yesterdays. This is our strength for tomorrow!

Many of the individuals who moved away had improved or different opportunities with relocation and resettlement. From their new settlements, they branched out into all of society. Many were glad to conceal or forget their identity. They were still dark, but other people often didn't perceive them as a threat in less noticeable concentrations. Their often pleasing and opposite features, compared to their pale neighbors, added to their mystique, attraction, and dissolution. In small, isolated numbers, they were frequently pursued as mates without even concern for their former deprived background. For example, my very fair-skinned father married my dark mother without a clue of her, with the exception of the knowledge that she was from Tennessee. He died not knowing of Newman's Ridge, the term Melungeon, or any of its connotations. As Henry Price said in reference to their dissolution, "Two enemies they could not overcome—time and the attractiveness of their womenfolk to the surrounding white settlers."[1]

When one knows their story and heritage, they can still be found in diluted numbers throughout our society. I initially learned of my

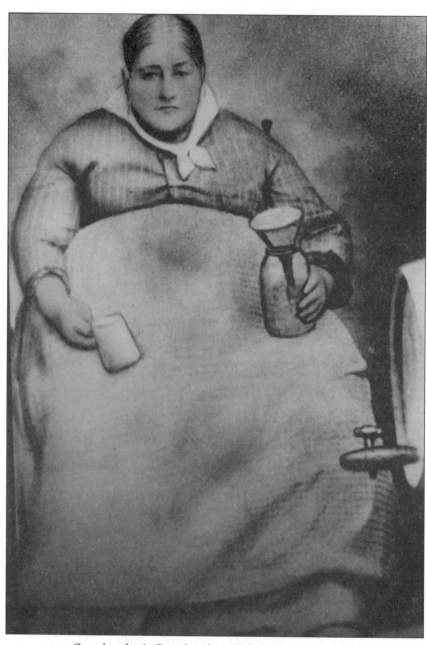

Grandmother's Grandmother, Mahala Collins Mullins.
Courtesy of Grandmother Hattie Mullins Bales (deceased)

heritage by seeing an article showing a picture of my great-great-grandmother. Her name and connection was unknown, but her picture had always been on the dresser of my grandmother. Upon tying the article to the dresser picture, and in spite of the denial of my mother, a mission was launched. Since my first enlightenment, I have been aware of their presence and have found them in many places.

Even today, when one listens for key names and checks physical features and origins of selected people as remnants of a minority, they are among us. Below is Don Bell, a member of the First Presbyterian Church of Rochelle, Illinois. He has the right name, as many Bells were in the Newman's Ridge area. He has the right features, with graying black hair, dark skin, and black eyes. With these telltale factors in mind, he was asked of his origin. He said his father was from Missouri, and that was immediately a red flag. Later he was asked about his grandfather. He checked and found his grandfather to be from somewhere in East Tennessee. The pieces of the puzzle all fit, and he was told the story of the Melungeons. He was fascinated and went to tell his wife of his new discovery. She was not enthused about him having a dark-skinned and mountainous background, as she preferred him being what she knew to be German.

At our next meeting, he reported that he was German and not

The Bell Family.
Courtesy of Loretta and Don Bell

Ernest Perkins.
Frankfort High School Yearbook-
1949
Courtesy of Ernest Perkins

Melungeon. We talked of his Melungeon heritage, and once again, he converted to being a proud Melungeon. Look around you for appropriate names and features, as they are still here and sometimes hidden among us.[2]

Another individual appeared in my hometown of Frankfort, Indiana, who was dark, with straight black hair and "tawny" skin. His last name was Perkins. The Perkins name is another in the annals of Melungia. It is not found in the Newman's Ridge area, but is a connection in other known Melungeon areas. His features were Caucasian, he was very athletic, and, as a result of his attributes, he was popular with the opposite sex. Unfortunately, Ernest Perkins was not allowed in the local public swimming pool in the 1950s for he was labeled a Negro. He was also denied dental care in the all-white town.

The local historical society in my retirement town sponsored a Melungeon program. Local people did not know much about the term Melungeon, but saw the notice of the meeting in the local paper. On the eve of the meeting, the president of the society noticed a group of 15-20 dark people milling nervously in the rear of the room. I was sent to their area and approached the people for a welcoming and introduction. When asked their names, several replied, "Collins." Thus launched the discovery of more local Melungeons as well as unknown kin. This was not totally unexpected and a joy, as my chosen retirement area is within fifty miles of my mother's and her neighbors' original relocation from Tennessee.

In general, if one travels within the junctions of the tristate core area of Tennessee, Virginia, and North Carolina, degrees of dark features will be very prevalent in the populace. There are many large areas with dark-eyed, dark-haired people in abundance. Probably most have no idea of their lost heritage.

Of course, a place such as Sneedville, Tennessee, has a very high percentage of dark people. To verify such an observation, just sit in a local restaurant for an hour to see all the versions of the descendants of Newman's Ridge and the surrounding environs. Some even appear, with their blond hair of choice, but with the telltale dark eyes and skin.

It is difficult to generalize or trace the many who migrated out of Hancock County and were absorbed in the society of the majority. We do know that many were educated and became leaders and outstanding citizens for their communities, while some others did not survive the scars of their past. How have those fared that remained in their ancestral home of Hancock County?

The area has changed. Many non-Melungeons have retired or live in the area. Land values and the cost of living have been low enough to attract people from distant places. The agricultural potential is low, but the scenery is superb. Again, we must generalize, as many of the natives are the leaders of Hancock County, but as a whole, those that stayed in their original area and did not pursue additional outside opportunities did not all fare as well.

Let us examine the situation through the overall economics of Hancock County. We must keep in mind that most Melungeons have been absorbed or moved away, but many scattered remnants and diluted genes still exist throughout the county population. With this fact in mind, the wealth indicators of 1983-1986 had Hancock County in 95 place of 95 counties of Tennessee. In 1987, Hancock had raised to 94th, with Picket County in 95th place. Hancock was at $7,005 per capita with Picket at $6,934.

At the time of this study, Hancock County had a population of 6,800 with a work force of 3,050, and half working outside the county. Unemployment was listed at 5.2% verses a national rate of 5.0 %. In 1980, unemployment reached 10.82% and climbed to 15.69% in 1984.[3]

In 1999, Hancock County was back at the economic bottom of the counties of Tennessee. Income per capita was one half the U. S. average. Farming and industry contributed less than ten percent to the income of the county, and one half the work force still must drive to another county to find employment. Local students receive the least amount of funds per student in the state, although test scores are far from last. Prior to a new missionary group that was started in 1991, there were no parks, recreation, or programs for youth outside the school.[4]

The infrastructure still fares no better than many of the individuals, as the school system has been in dire financial straits many times. In 1991, many newspaper articles covered the Hancock County school budget problems. The system eliminated extended contracts, textbook purchases, guidance counselors, special skill, staff, physical education, teacher's free time, and sixth and seventh grade teaching positions. During that year, money was only available for transportation through December.

In this crisis period, the community responded with all volunteer painting, cleaning, and maintenance of the school properties. Fund-raisers were held to pay for everything from telephone bills to bar soap and toilet tissue. The families sold candy and doughnuts, had ice cream socials, rummage sales, and sponsored barbecues; also turkey and spaghetti suppers and tractor pulls.[5]

Such stories have plagued the community intermittently throughout their post-missionary history. Opportunities and resources are limited, but the people seem to survive and trudge on with perseverance and hope. The newest missionaries are now the Methodists, and they are a part of the Jubilee program.

What happened to the Presbyterians in this era? They are gone! There is not one Presbyterian church left in the county! The Methodist Church is prospering as are several Baptist. Of particular interest to our story is Elm Springs Baptist Church, at the base of Newman's Ridge and at the end of Vardy Valley (Snake Hollow), where Shepard" Buck Gibson's descendant, Delmont (Seven) Gibson (page 151), preaches the gospel. The Holiness churches are back in force, as many earlier Melungeons were inclined toward the more fundamental Christian religions prior to Presbyterianism. The serpent handling and strychnine drinking has returned along with the standard Holiness rituals.

Pastor Henry Swiney, who has preached in the area for over fifty years, has led a good group of devoted Christians through the steps of being saved, testimonials, foot washings, serpent handling, and

The Jubilee Project.
Courtesy of Steven Hodges

The Scriptural Charge. Courtesy of Bill Snead.

The Serpents. Courtesy of Bill Snead.

the many revivals to strengthen their faith.[6] His emotionalism is effective for their faith and inspiring to outsiders to the Holiness doctrine. I have deep roots to Reverend Swiney as Swiney and my sociopathic Uncle Connor were longtime friends in rowdiness before Swiney was saved in his early twenties.

Note the picture on page 246 of the Swiney brothers and their large size for the time. Henry was probably 6'2", weighed 225 pounds, and spoke of participating in four to five fights on the courthouse lawn of Sneedville in the early days on a Sunday afternoon. He told of fighting side by side with my uncle, Connor Bales, who was six foot tall and weighed 230-240. Swiney was once asked if the two large men ever fought each other. Swiney replied, "Oh no, we were close friends; we felt together we could whoop anyone!" More than likely they were both strong and feared each other, but they knew together the odds were that they could defeat any pair of smaller opponents.

The standard Holiness church services are on Wednesday and Saturday night. I have had the occasion to visit members of the congregation in their homes on days prior to that evening's church. The discussion on these days always centers around the church and the statement," If you love me, you will go to church with me tonight." This statement is not to be made light of, excused, or debated, as these people are devoted to their church and their God. Their kin and friends are expected to go to church with them. I have always obeyed their expectations out of respect and love for them and their beliefs.

I have also attended the Swiney services on snake nights with the explicit instructions to Reverend Swiney, "No snakes in my pews, please!" The request was always respected, and the entire congregation, including visitors, always left the service with a deeper sense of reverence for the Godhead. Their faith is deep and sincere, and those outsiders who have been privileged to attend their services feel a different allegiance to their own religion.

The Swineys were not Melungeons, but lived among them. Reverend Henry married one of the group, Kitty Gibson. He is now 89 years of age and retired, but as recently as 1988, I witnessed his services and those of his younger associate, Reverend Gerald Fleener, who was bitten shortly after a visitation. Young Fleener

The Swiney Brothers. Courtesy of Macie Mullins.

e victim's kin lacked faith

" *I don't pay any attention to getting bit. I never have been to a hospital or even a doctor. He probably would have been all right if his mother hadn't gotten scared.* **"**

The Rev. Henry Swiney
Minister of the Sneedville Holiness Church

The News – Reverend Fleener
The Citizen Tribune of Morristown[7]

was eventually transported to the University of Tennessee hospital in Knoxville and recovered. The papers were abuzz with the event. Henry Swiney was interviewed and quoted throughout the area. He has never been arrested for his religious activities.

How are Melungeons accepted in the core area today? The process has been slow. Better roads and vehicles necessitated their association with people outside the clan. The children all came to Sneedville to school after the closing of the mission school. Communication has helped to break down barriers.

The Melungeons were basically mountain people, and people of the highlands and mountain people have been known to be deficient in their willingness to commend a person openly for a favor done or the recognition of any desirable skill or trait. As with other highland or mountain people, the Melungeons have been deprived of compliments and any type of appreciation. Their situation was even more accentuated, because they were also the outcasts of the highlands.[8] These types of cultural quirks have certainly slowed any rapid acceptance.

One event in the 1960s did have a positive effect on the Melungeons. A few researchers began to study them as a unique, but different people, and wrote more favorable reports concerning their heritage. Carson-Newman College sponsored and performed an outdoor drama in Sneedville written entirely about Melungeons. The play depicted Melungeons in a good light, and suddenly, the group became an asset to a community in deep need of something to generate increased financial respectability. The drama was well-written and exposed many more outside people to the long history of the colony. It lasted seven seasons, but closed due to the remoteness of Sneedville, inadequate lodging, limited capital returns, and the erosion of good promotional management. It was another favorable step in the acceptance of the reclusive people.[9]

A different type of phenomena that is favorable to the remnants of the colony is the trend toward being a "wantabe" Melungeon. Today, in the general area, there are many "wantabe" Melungeons among the populations of the three-state area, particularly the more prosperous or educated people, who are searching for a concept that would allow them to be different and unique. People who were lucky enough to have missed the suffering and discrimination of the past have suddenly discovered the possibility of being part of a small group who are being studied for all their many implications, and sometimes proudly become "wantabe" Melungeons. Most people in this category must have a good sense of self-esteem and confidence in themselves in order to pursue this new role.

This same situation has occurred, and is still occurring in the world of the Native American. They were also exploited and denied their heritage, until people who never experienced their demise decided the concept of being a minority was romantic. "Wantabe" Indians in the author's community now wear headbands, beads, and Native American regalia and usually claim some limited degree of being of Indian descent. They attend powwows with expensive, authentic Native American costumes, and dance authentic dances in memory of some sacred Indian forefather who was probably killed by their own actual white forefathers.

They ignore the fact that their white forefathers supplied vast amounts of alcohol or smallpox-infested blankets to destroy entire populations. They do not know of the passing of the great tribes of the Yuchi and Mandan. They do not want to know that these great civilizations have passed from history to oblivion under the onslaught of the western progression by the whites. Most do not know about the missing information in their white history books that was deleted by discrimination.

What happened to the Melungeon people of the twentieth century who actually experienced similar ethnic cleansing as the Native Americans? The few that are still alive today are not overjoyed with their new acceptance and the current popularity of their colony. Many become irritated and withdrawn if they sense "outsider" curiosity about their people as isolated or different from the norm. Even today, Clara Belle Miser Horton, an Indiana transplant, gets angry when the word Melungeon or its connotations, are mentioned. She has been observed closing her eyes, to shut an entire group out of her world when the word or material pertaining to them as interesting, unique, or different is mentioned.

Hughie Mullins (now deceased) was so sensitive that he would depart abruptly at the mention of the word Melungeon. He would leave a person stranded in the woods at the very mention of the idea. He would say, "If you're gonna talk about them Lungeons,

I'm goin home!"

Ollie Bales would always say, "Why you wanna talk about them ole people, they's all dead?" She would worry about my sanity when Melungeons were brought up for discussion. She would tell her grandchildren, "Jimmie's off his rocker, talkin about them ole people in Tennessee. That job's gettin to his brain!" She never returned to Vardy Valley after leaving in 1931 until her death in 1988. I never knew or saw my great-grandmother (page 202), who died on the Clinch in the 1950s.

Will we ever find the origin of these people? Possibly undiscovered documents or writings that are not currently available or translatable may be found or deciphered. An even better hope of discovering the source of the Melungeons may be through archaeology, and even it has its human problems. A continual search for new facts requires resources to be available for us to a find a successful answer. To continue to progress in the quest, deterrents such as apathy and resistance to change must be eliminated.

For example, a recent editorial in a local paper spoke of the oldest Americans arriving from more than one place. The article reiterated the dogma of Americans crossing the Bering Strait 12,000 years ago on the land bridge from Siberia to Alaska. It spoke of additional, prehistoric human remains being found recently with the skulls being different than those of Mongoloid or Native American.

The article reported that these newer archaeological finds were below what were thought to be the earliest human settlements. More artifacts and remains were found in these areas, which didn't fit the physiological features of modern Native Americans. The article then commented that archaeologists have been reluctant to report these startling new finds for fear of being labeled "crackpots." The editorial mentioned *Newsweek* being bold enough to devote a major article to the subject.

The commentary then spoke of the Native Americans who may not like the repucussions of such a discovery for fear of losing first rights to any government programs. It spoke of their fear of the loss of first rights and privileges to native remains being held in museums. The editorial even covered the possibility of white supremacists responding to the finding of 12,000-year-old Caucasoid remains in North America with, "them thievin' Injuns stole our land."

The editorial ended with the potential for a good, new feeling of the racial diversity of having mixed ancestors. It spoke of America being a melting pot today that draws strength and flexibility from the variety of its populace, as it has since its first settlement.[10]

One would expect the paper to receive many letters as a result of such an editorial. Amazingly, people were so apathetic to the ideas that not one letter was published in response to such a controversial editorial. This was the featured editorial in the town of Bloomington, Indiana, home of Indiana University, an educational institution where almost every statement becomes a subject of heated debate! Apparently, we do not want to debate or consider change for our history books—regardless of the evidence for a different past! Apathy and resistance contribute to the denial of funds and energy toward progress.

Another deterrent to the role of archaeology in the discovery of origins of possible unknown continental people is ego. As interest grows in the subject, "wantabe" Melungeons need to find something new and unique to their own cause. Altered data, transplanted data, and unscientific information are the follies of individual attempts to be recognized. In our pursuit, we must always weigh each new theory and never fail to use scientific procedures. All can participate, but outlandish new finds or reports must first be judged by the integrity and credentials of the reporter.

On an even larger scale, new archaeological sites and sources could hold clues to new Melungeon information, but nationalism, or the desire of individual nations to say "we" were here first, or "we" were civilized before you were, can lead to contamination of archaeological facts. For example, in the 1930s and 40s, many artifacts found outside Germany proper were interpreted as early Germanic and became just cause for evictions or slaughters in the name of the mother country. In this era, the power and prestige of America is reason enough to motivate any country to want to claim early connections through the Melungeons or others. We must beware of nations claiming discovery of America based on these thoughts.

Even religion, under the guise of archaeology, is not exempt as a deterrent in our search for more information. Martin Luther once said, "What harm would it do if a man told a good, strong lie for the sake of the good and for the Christian Church... a useful lie, a helpful lie, such lies would not be against God; he would accept them." This premise in relation to religion could even solve the Melungeon mystery in the hands of the right powers with the wrong motives.

The desire of some for a more romantic past, particularly in the case of the Melungeons, also harms the facts. Many want to interpret the scratches on every rock to symbolize their favorite theory of the source of the Melungeons. Some of the artifacts, as we have seen in our study, do have ancient messages. We must be sure that those who might know the translations are not biased.

Finally, the problem with our dependence upon archaeologists is the plain instability of some proponents of the studies. As we recall, some give no credence to a find unless it is by a professional. Lay people certainly must use caution in their explorations for possible artifacts, but there is too much material to investigate and too few archaeologists. We must work with them and not for them. People battle the ego over true knowledge, and crazy people have crazy claims.[11] This pearl can apply to the professional or to the layman.

Having made the above qualifications to the weaknesses of archaeology, it still may hold the key to the origin of the Melungeons and others.

We know if Welsh chain mail were to be found in a cave on Newman's Ridge we would have a good clue to an origin. Perhaps even a Spanish sword plus some accompanying coins in another area would prove the source of other people. Many sites in the area have not been explored and still may hold the secret of the Melungeons. The only hope is that future unscrupulous people do not follow this tenet of the unexplored and invade the area to disrupt the privacy of the people of Vardy Valley. This concept can be taken farther. With the technology of new detectors that can see under the ground, we will find unforseen information. By this same token, better detectors under the sea will find stunning archaeological evidence of our history. Thus far, treasure hunters have worked to find riches. Perhaps we will eventually find a Welsh ship in American waters.

We must also give credence to Pollitzer and others who have prioneered in gene work. We have just now mapped the human DNA. Just think of how we will eventually be able to create migratory pat-

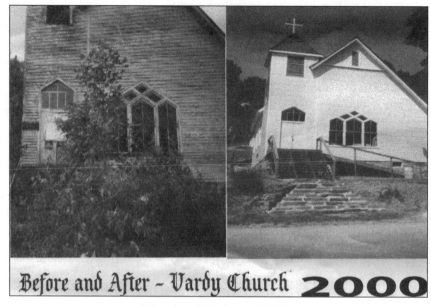

The Church-Before and After.
Courtesy of the Vardy Community Historical Society, Inc.

terns of peoples and isolate particular groups by understanding our genes.

For the moment, we must leave the unsolved origin of the Melungeon story to the scientists and archaeologists, but the discrimination is still very tangible.

There has been a very recent revival of pride in the heritage of Vardy Valley with the restoration of the 1899 Presbyterian Church. The church is now used as a gathering place for the Vardy Community Historical Society. The school could not be saved, but long hours of labor and money from a group of former students has restored the church to its early glory.

Three reunions have been held in the newly renovated church, and attendance has been in the range of 200 per session. The pride was evident, and all former students were in good spirits and enjoyed the meetings. We grow stronger when we feel good about ourselves and our past.

The last meeting, held in October, 1999, carried the theme "An Old Fashioned Hard Candy Christmas." We must qualify that these former students that were in attendance lived near the end of the

Proud Memories.
The Program

Vardy Alumni Reunion
October 16, 1999

Welcome .... Troy L. Williams

Prayer .... R. C. Mullins

Lunch

Christmas Remembered	**3:00 PM**
Introduction .... W. C. Collins	**Museum Dedication**
The Christmas Story .... Rev. Delmont Gibson	Introduction .... DruAnna Overbay
Hymn .... Away In A Manger	Guest .... Cherel Henderson
Hardy Candy .... Santa's Helpers	East TN Historical Society
Closing Comments .... Vardy Alumni	Pictorial Story .... Dr. C. M. Lipsey
Prayer .... Rev. David Swartz	

Hard Candy Christmas.
Courtesy of the Committee

long, successful missionary period; therefore, they should have enjoyed the maximum results of the program for both themselves and their community. The alumni met, ate lunch, and enjoyed a program complete with a giant decorated cedar tree. There were speakers, and later in the program, former students extemporaneously spoke fondly of their Christmas memories in the church.

The speakers talked about the various missionary standards for the Christmas distributions: Students were to attend the church in order to get any Christmas gifts. Those with very limited resources and not enough money to dress warmly would only get clothes. Those with some resources would receive some toys depending upon family status.

All gifts of clothes and toys were shipped from the parent church in New York. Items were locally sorted by need for each family. Selected achievers helped in the large sorting project, and sorters frequently struggled with their own desires to possess certain toys, but followed the charitable sharing guidelines of the minister.

All members received one small container of hard candy; thus, the theme, "An Old Fashioned Hard Candy Christmas." This candy was very coveted, as most did not get any candy all year save this individual portion from the missionaries. After the session, one of the outsider university attendees asked me, "Would you say these are the elite of the remnants of the colony?" The answer was, "Yes. These were of the latter stages of a long and successful missionary era. Unfortunately, others did not survive any part of the entire concept. They are not here and do not share this joy!"

This same core group of people who believe in their heritage are now planning to move the Mahala Mullin's home down from Newman's Ridge to a spot across from the church.

Some say background is a matter of time, place, and luck; our achievement is what we do with it.[12] We see this philosophy at work in the Vardy Church. We must instill this in all our future descendants if we are to survive and prosper.

Psalms 1 vs. 3   We are like trees
planted by the streams of water,
which yield our fruit in its season,
and our leaves do not whither.

In all that we do we prosper.

O Hail Melungo !

[1] Henry Price, *Melungeons: The Vanishing Colony of Newman's Ridge*, Hancock County Drama Association, 1971.

[2] Interviews with Don and Loretta Bell, Rochelle, Illinois, 1985.

[3] *The Citizen Tribune*, "Hancock County Out of Income Cellar," Morristown, Tennessee, June, 1987.

[4] Statistics from broshure of Jubilee Project, Inc., Sneedville, Tennessee, Steve Hodges, Director.

[5] *The Citizen Tribune*, " Hancock County Community Helps School With No Money," Morristown, Tennessee, August, 29, 1991.

[6] Thomas Burton, *Serpent Handling Believers*, The University of Tennessee Press, Knoxville, Tennessee, 1993.

[7] Betsy Kauffman, News Sentinel, "Church members say snake victum's kin lacked faith." Citizen Tribune, Morristown, Tennessee, November, 1988

[8] Harry M. Caudill, *Night Comes to the Cumberlands*, Boston: Little, Brown, 1962.

[9] Thomas Q. Zachary, "The Melungeons, A Review of History and Change," University of Tennessee, Knoxville, Tennessee, 1972.

[10] *Sunday Herald Times*, "Americas racially diverse from start," Bloomington, Indiana,April 25, 1999.

[11] Kenneth L. Freder, *Frauds, Myths, and Mysteries*, Mayfield Publishing Company, Mountain View, California, 1999.

[12] Cyrus H. Gordon, *Before Columbus*, Crown Publishers, Inc. New York, New York, 1971.